GW01459894

Collins
Science Plus +

2

SECOND EDITION

Published by HarperCollins*Publishers* Limited
77–85 Fulham Palace Road
Hammersmith
London
W6 8JB

Browse the complete Collins catalogue at
www.collinseducation.com

© HarperCollins*Publishers* Ltd 2004

10 9 8 7 6 5 4 3 2 1

ISBN 0 00 716076 3

Gareth Price and Martin Davies assert their moral rights to be identified as the authors of this work.

British Library Cataloguing in Publication Data
A Catalogue record for this publication is available from the British Library

Designed by Chi Leung
Project Management by Nicola Tidman
Picture research by Caroline Thompson
Illustrations by Phillip Burrows and Peter Harper
Production by Sarah Robinson
Printed and bound by Scotprint Haddington East Lothian

1st edition writing team
Elizabeth Forth
Jenny Jones
Bob McDuell
Shirley Parsons
Gareth Price
Pamela Singh
Linda Welds

Illustrations from 1st edition by Barking Dog Art, Russell Birkett, Tom Cross, Jerry Fowler

You may also like to visit:
www.harpercollins.co.uk
The book lover's website

Acknowledgements

Every effort has been made to contact the holders of copyright material, but if any have been inadvertently overlooked the publishers will be pleased to make the necessary arrangements at the first opportunity.

The publishers would like to thank the following for permission to reproduce photographs (T = Top, B = Bottom, C = Centre, L= Left, R = Right):

Action Plus/Phillippe Millereau, 55;
www.JohnBirdsall.co.uk, 13;
Courtesy of Blackpool Pleasure Beach, 12;
Anthony Blake Photo Library/Maximilian, 17, Graham Kirk, 23;
Martyn Chillmaid, 54, 56C, 57B, 58B, 59, 66;
www.codetection.com, 53B;
Corbis/James L Amos, 7C, Peter Peterson, 19, Lloyd Cluff, 38;
Derby Evening Telegraph, 49C;
Ecoscene/Paul Thompson, 40;
Eye Ubiquitous/John Dakers, 20T;
Firepix International Photo Library/Tony Myers F.R.P.S, 4;
Fortean Picture Library/A Radford, 45;
Tony Waltham – Geophotos, 36L, 37L, 61, 67, 79, 83T;
Getty Images/Matthew Stockman, 35, Jon Buckle, 76;
Getty Images, 32, 43, 47L;
With thanks to Granada Television, 53L;
Ronald Grant Archive, 28, Allied Artists, 27, New Line Cinema, 25, 29, Rank/Carlton, 57T, Caralco Pictures, 72;
Sally & Richard Greenhill Photo Library, 53R;
Kobal Collection/Icon/Ladd/Paramount, 16, Columbia/Tristar/Jack English, 24T, Columbia/Darren Michaels, 26, 20th Century Fox, 41, Warner Bros, 64;
Nature Picture Library/Brandon Cole, 9;
NHPA/Brian Hawkes, 48, David Woodfall, 49T, ANT, 60;
OSF/Paul Franklin, 8, Harold Taylor, 9(inset), Deni Bown, 18TL, Geoff Kidd, 18TC;
PA Photos, 7T;
Tom Pfieffer/www.decadevolcano.net, 39;
Redferns/David Redfern, 5, Hayley Madden, 71, Martin Philbey, 81T;
Rex Features Ltd, 14, 37C, 62, 65, 68, 74, 75;
Science Photo Library, 85, Alain Dex, Publiphoto Diffusion, 6, Dept of Clinical Radiology, Salisbury District Hospital, 7B, Robert Brook, 10, Martin Bond, 11L, 50, David Nunuk, 11C, Alex Bartel, 11R, Dr Jurgen Scriba, 15, Manfred Kage, 20C, David Solzberg, 21T, Noble Proctor, 21C, John Heseltine, 22, Will & Deni McIntyre, 24L(background), David Parker, 33, Francoise Sauze, 34, Philippe Plailly, 46, 86, James King-Holmes, 51, Simon Fraser, 52, G Brad Lewis, 56T, Claude Nuridsany & Marie Perennou, 57C, Colin Cuthbert, 58TR, John Sanford, 58TL, Maximilian Stock Ltd, 69, TRL Ltd, 78, James Stevenson, 81C, Hank Morgan, 83B;
SHOUT, 36T, 47R;
Skyscan/Ian Pillinger, 77;
Still Pictures/David Hoffman, 37T, John Maier 44, Donald Tipton, 70, Mark Edwards, 73;
Stockfile/Steve Behr, 42;
C&S Thompson, 80.

Cover image: Subatomic Particles – Science Photo Library/Mehau Kulyk.

Contents

Contents

1.1 A vital gas

Most people are not killed by the flames in a fire. It is the fumes and lack of **oxygen** that do the damage. That is why firefighters wear breathing apparatus in burning buildings. The cylinders contain compressed air. Inside fire engines there are cylinders of oxygen ready for **casualties** who have difficulty breathing because their lungs have been damaged by smoke.

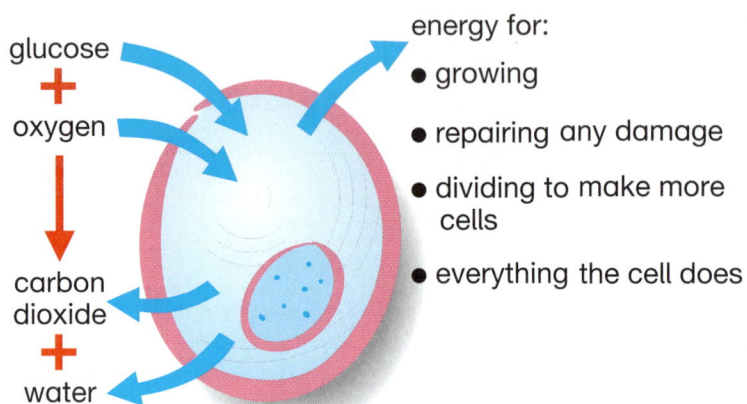

glucose
+
oxygen

carbon dioxide
+
water

energy for:
- growing
- repairing any damage
- dividing to make more cells
- everything the cell does

But why do we need oxygen? Every cell in your body needs **energy**. The **glucose** from food reacts with the oxygen to provide energy. This process is called **respiration**.

Glucose + oxygen → energy + carbon dioxide + water

The water and **carbon dioxide** are waste products. You get rid of them when you breathe out. On a cold day you can see the moisture in your breath. You cannot see the carbon dioxide because it is a colourless gas.

1 What kills most people in fires?
2 Why do firefighters carry oxygen in their fire engines?
3 Where does the glucose in the cells of the body come from?
4 What is produced when glucose reacts with oxygen?

**oxygen   casualties   energy   glucose   respiration
carbon dioxide**

Air sac
Oxygen goes from the air into the bloodstream. Carbon dioxide goes the other way.

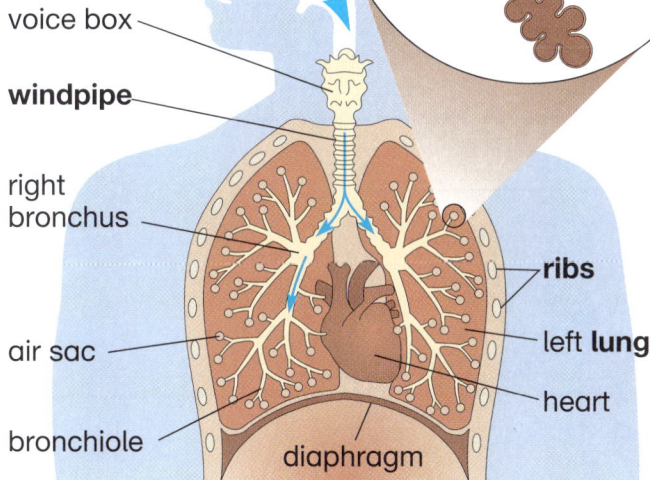

voice box

windpipe

right bronchus

air sac

bronchiole

diaphragm

ribs

left **lung**

heart

1.2 A nice pair of lungs

You need a good set of lungs for this! Actually, it is the muscles attached to your ribs that allow you to breathe in and out.

Not everyone's lungs can hold the same amount of air. An average man can hold 5–6 litres of air in his lungs. A fit athlete may hold up to 7 litres. A child would have a smaller lung capacity.

Breathing in
Air is sucked into the lungs.

Ribs pull the lungs upwards and outwards.

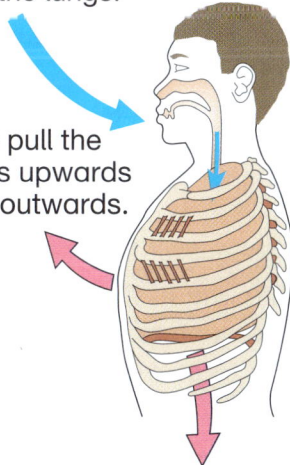

Muscles pull the lungs downwards.

Breathing out
Air is squeezed out of the lungs.

Ribs squeeze the lungs by pushing downwards and inwards.

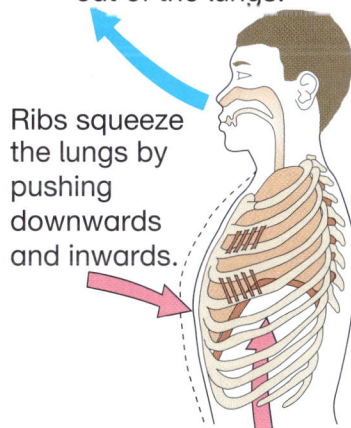

The stomach pushes on the lungs from below.

1 Which direction do the ribs move in when someone breathes out?
2 What is the name of the tube that carries air from your mouth to your lungs?
3 What happens to the air when it reaches the air sacs?
4 Draw a flow chart to show how air gets from the mouth to the air sacs in the lungs.

windpipe   lungs   air sac

In an asthmatic person the walls swell narrowing the airway. During an asthma attack, the muscle fibres squeeze the airways even more.

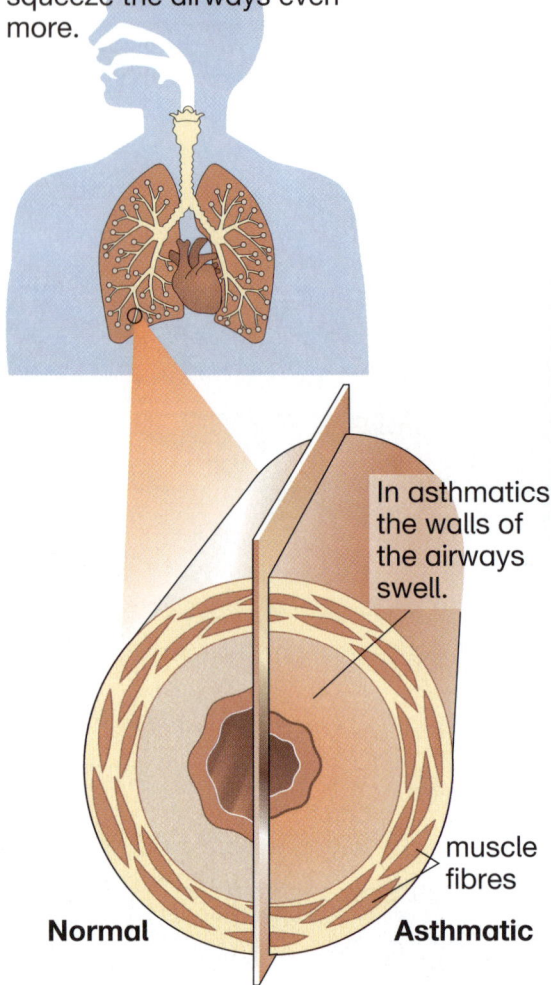

In asthmatics the walls of the airways swell.

muscle fibres

Normal   **Asthmatic**

1.3 Fighting for breath

This girl has **asthma**. Asthma stops a person breathing in and out properly. The **symptoms** that people with asthma have are coughing, wheezing and being short of breath.

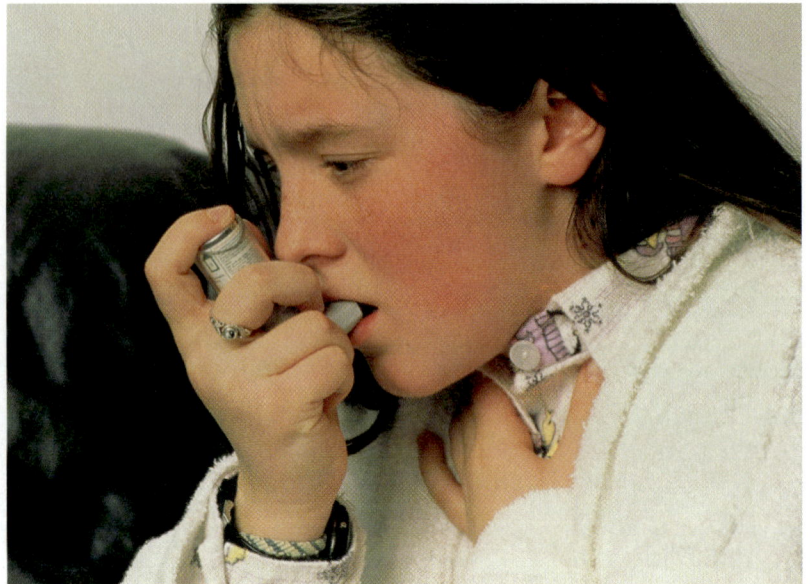

Asthma reduces:
- the speed that people can breathe in and out, and
- the total volume of air the lungs can hold.

This is because the walls of the airways swell, so the space for air is reduced. The airways get even narrower during exercise or if the air is polluted.

People with asthma may need to use an **inhaler** like the one in the picture above. There are two types of inhaler – **relievers** and **preventers**. The doctor may also prescribe drugs that are **protectors**. They help to prevent another attack.

Type of inhaler	What does it do?
Reliever	Relieves the symptoms. Makes breathing easier.
Preventer	Reduces the swelling in the airways. Patient feels better.

1 Describe what happens to the airways of people with asthma.
2 Why do people with asthma need inhalers?
3 Design a poster for the wall of a sports centre which explains the symptoms of asthma.

asthma   symptom   inhaler   reliever   preventer
protector

1.4 Smoking

These protesters feel very strongly about smoking. They feel that smoking has such a bad affect on peoples' health that it should be banned from all public places. On the 14th of February 2003, cigarette advertising was banned in the UK.

☠ **Tar** – this clogs the lungs reducing their volume and the speed that people can breathe in and out. Colds, **bronchitis** and lung diseases are much more likely.

☠ Carbon monoxide – a poisonous gas which stops red blood cells carrying oxygen.

☠ **Nicotine** – an **addictive** drug that raises the heart rate.

☠ Hydrogen cyanide – a poisonous gas, used to execute condemned prisoners in the USA.

The arrow in the X-ray below points to a **cancer** in the lung. Scientists have proved that certain chemicals in **tobacco** smoke cause cancer and **heart disease**. That's why there is a warning on every cigarette packet about the dangers of smoking.

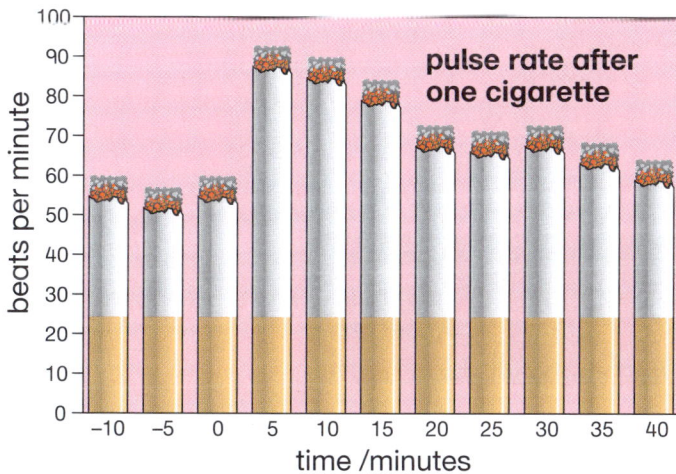

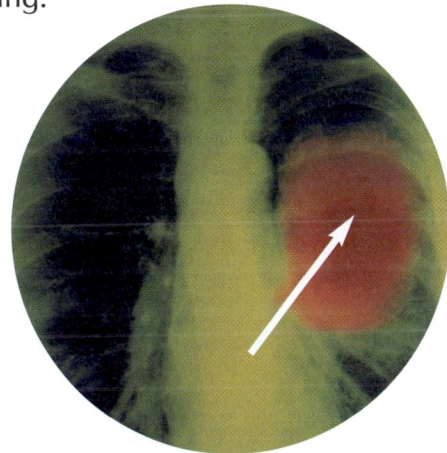

pulse rate after one cigarette

Although people who smoke know that it is harmful, they often cannot stop. This means that they put their lives at risk every time they smoke. People who do not smoke may be '**passive**' smokers if they live with people who smoke.

1 Design a poster warning people of the dangers of smoking.
2 Your friend has asked you to help him to stop smoking. How would you do this?
3 List three dangerous chemicals found in tobacco smoke.

cancer	tobacco	heart disease	tar
bronchitis	nicotine	addictive	passive smoking

2.1 Green spaces

We all tried to catch small fish in a pond when we were young. The trouble is, it was often easier to catch beetles, worms, pondweed and rubbish! Even a small pond or stream contains lots of different **organisms**. How do biologists remember what they are called?

Biologists use a **key** to work out the name of different organisms from the characteristics they can see.

The carbon cycle

Plants may not be the most exciting organisms, but they are very important. Life on earth would not exist without them. Plants make their own food from the **carbon dioxide** in the air. This food making process is called **photosynthesis**.

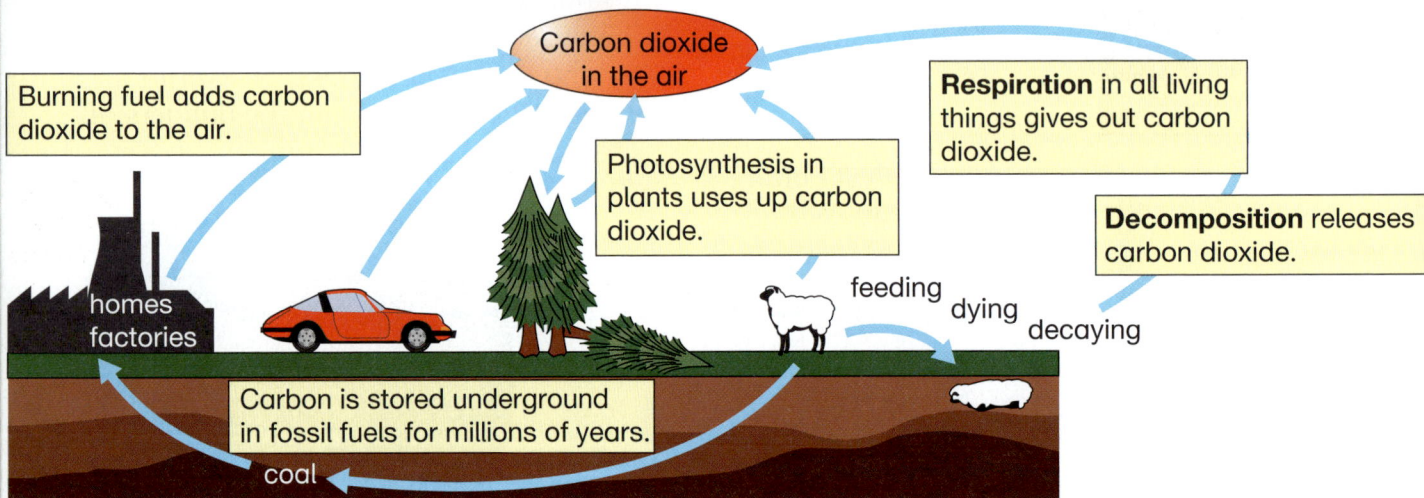

Burning fuel adds carbon dioxide to the air.

Respiration in all living things gives out carbon dioxide.

Carbon dioxide in the air

Photosynthesis in plants uses up carbon dioxide.

Decomposition releases carbon dioxide.

feeding

dying

decaying

homes factories

Carbon is stored underground in fossil fuels for millions of years.

coal

Photosynthesis is part of the **carbon cycle**. Carbon is needed by all living things. Carbon moves through the food chain when animals eat plants and other animals. When plants and animals die, the carbon goes into the soil and is eventually released into the air as carbon dioxide gas. Carbon is also returned to the air when animals breathe out and when humans burn fossil fuels and wood.

1 What happens to the carbon in living things when they die?
2 What gas do animals breathe out?
3 Why do plants need carbon dioxide?
4 Why are plants so important to animals?

| organisms | key | carbon dioxide | photosynthesis |
| respiration | decomposition | carbon cycle | |

2.2 Food chains

Sharks are **carnivores** – they eat meat. But even the most ferocious shark depends on tiny green plants too small to see without a microscope. These tiny green plants, shown in the photograph, are **producers**. They use energy from the sun, water and carbon dioxide to make food. Producers are eaten by animals called **herbivores**. These herbivores are then eaten by bigger animals, which the shark will eat!

A **food chain** is a simple way to show what eats what. This diagram shows how lots of different food chains in a pond are linked. This is called a **food web**.

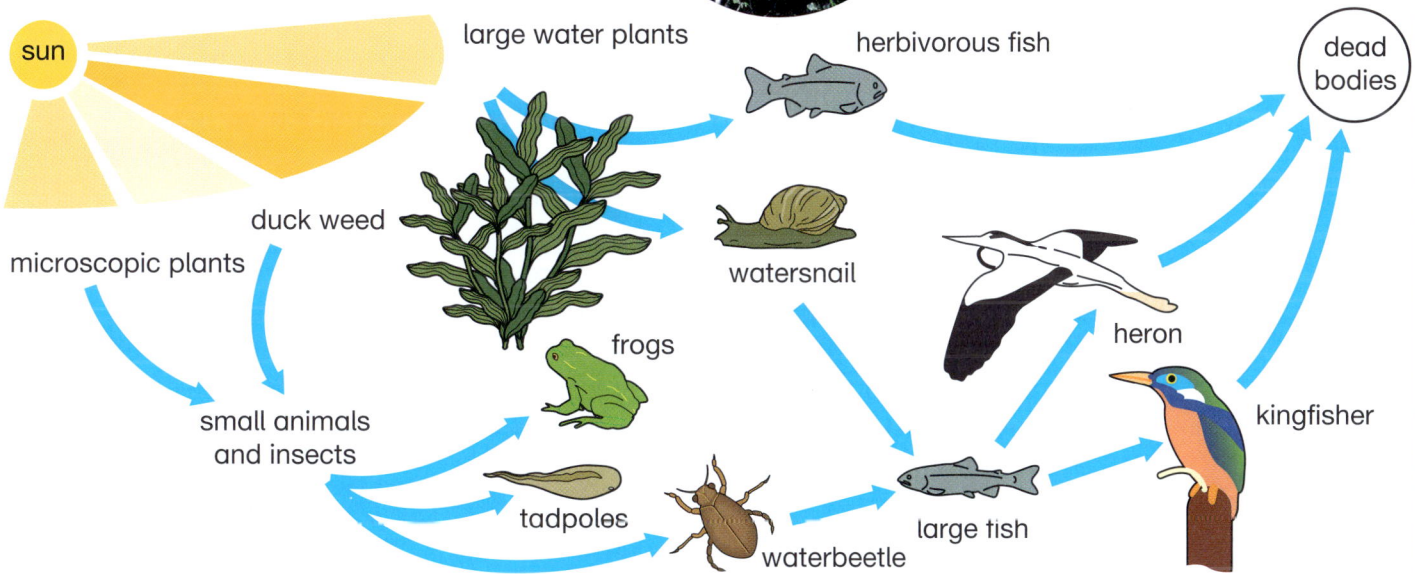

1. Write down one example of a food chain from the diagram above.
2. What is a producer? Put a box around the producer in your food chain.
3. What is a herbivore? Put a line under the herbivore in your food chain.
4. What is a carnivore? Put a star by the carnivore in your food chain.

carnivore **producer** **herbivore** **food chain** **food web**	

2.3 What a mess!

It's easy to see the problem here! Water can be **polluted** by rubbish, sewage, industrial chemicals and fertilisers. These **pollutants** are often poisonous to plants and animals.

Farmers sometimes use too much **fertiliser** on their fields. When this happens the extra fertiliser can run off into local streams and ponds, causing an increase in plant growth. Eventually there are so many plants that they block out the light and everything in the pond or stream dies.

You can find out if a pond or stream is polluted with chemicals by testing the water for **turbidity**. Turbid water is cloudy and so you cannot see through it. Turbidity is caused by suspended particles of dirt, which reduce plant growth. You can find out how much solid is present in the water by evaporating it to dryness. The solid left when all of the water has **evaporated** includes the **dissolved** chemicals.

1　List some of the things which pollute rivers, streams and ponds.
2　What happens when a stream becomes polluted with fertiliser?
3　Write a sentence to show what the word turbidity means.
4　Imagine that a local stream is badly polluted. Write a letter to your local council explaining how this has happened and why it is a problem. Say what you think should be done about it. Include diagrams in your report.

polluted	pollutants	fertiliser	turbidity
evaporate	dissolve		

Many of the products we use claim to be **environmentally friendly**. Environmentally friendly products tend to have very little **packaging** and the packaging can often be **recycled** to make new products. The best packaging is **reusable**. Milk bottles are collected, cleaned and reused. Other glass bottles may be taken to local bottle banks. Paper may be recycled. Toilet rolls are often made from recycled paper.

Transporting goods around takes up energy and can add to pollution. It may be more environmentally friendly to buy locally produced goods. Many things we buy are overpackaged. Every year we throw away lots of packaging. Some shops try to reduce this by encouraging customers to reuse their old carrier bags. Some products have the label 'This product has not been tested on animals'.

Organisations like Friends of the Earth and Greenpeace campaign to make people more aware of the needs of the planet. They encourage the government to create new laws to protect plants and animals. How could you encourage people to join in? And how could you make people care about environmental damage happening on the other side of the world?

1 What sort of things can be recycled?
2 What is the difference between recycling and reusing packaging?
3 List three things people can do to be more environmentally friendly.
4 Why are locally-produced goods more environmentally friendly than products from far away?

| environmentally friendly | packaging | recycle | reusable |

Fooling your senses

3.1 Balance – going for a ride

It's the biggest ride in Europe and thousands of people every year pay money to be shaken around and scared. It's bad enough if you're sick while you're on the ride, but think of the people below you in the fairground!

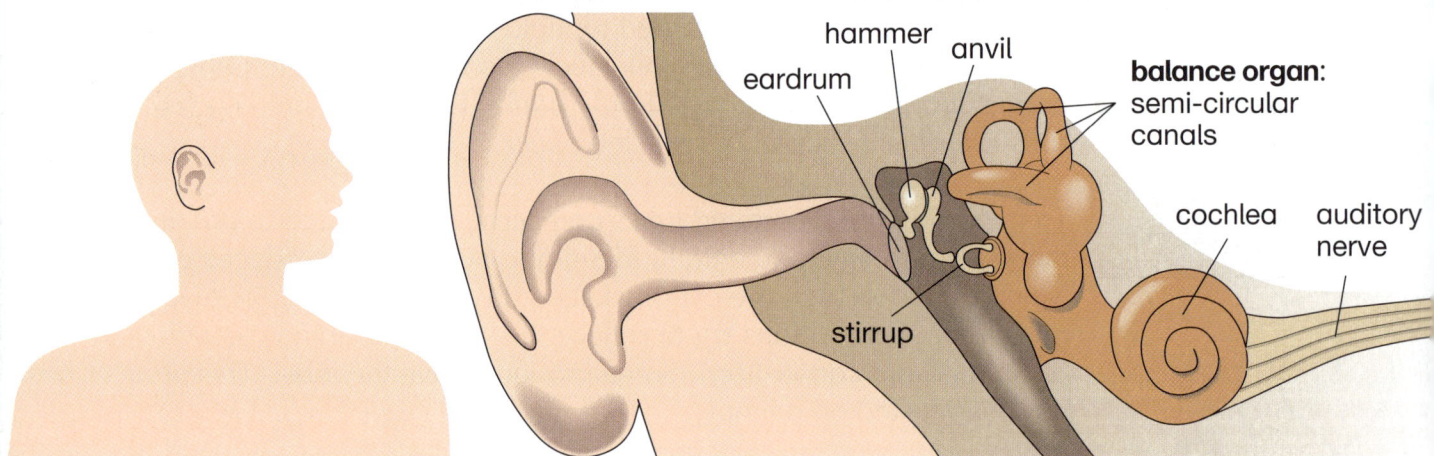

hammer anvil
eardrum
balance organ: semi-circular canals
cochlea auditory nerve
stirrup

In each of your ears you have an organ of **balance**. It tells your brain which way up you are and how you are moving. Each balance organ is made up of three small, fluid-filled tubes at right angles to each other. When you move, the fluid in the tubes moves – like the liquid in a spirit-level. This movement **stimulates sensory nerves** which send impulses to your brain. When you spin, the fluid picks up speed and continues to move even when you stop. Your brain interprets this as the ground moving and you feel giddy.

1 Where in the body are your balance organs?
2 What are the balance organs filled with?
3 Does the time you take to stop feeling giddy depend on how long you have been spinning? Plan an investigation to find out.

balance   stimulate   sensory nerves

3.2 Eating at the fair

Food usually smells good when it's cooking. People who sell snacks at fairs know that the smell of frying onions attracts people to buy hot dogs and burgers.

Your nose is sensitive to millions of different smells. As you breathe in, chemicals in the air dissolve in the moisture in your nose. The dissolved chemicals stimulate the nerves lining your nose. These nerves send information to your brain.

Taste and smell are very closely connected. If you have a cold you often cannot taste your food. This is because the sense cells in your nose cannot **detect** the chemicals through the mucus blocking your nose!

Your tongue has taste sensitive nerves called **taste buds**. You can only distinguish four tastes: sweet, sour, salt and bitter. So when you 'taste' delicious food, most of the flavour comes from the smell of the food. The taste buds for each taste are grouped in different parts of the tongue.

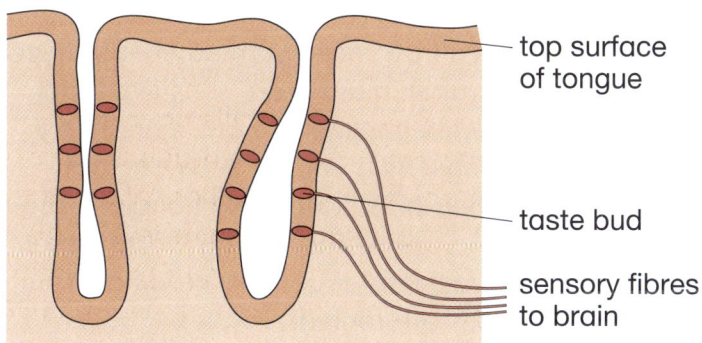

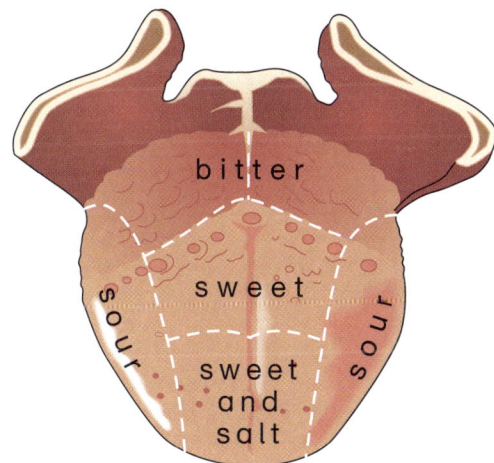

top surface of tongue

taste bud

sensory fibres to brain

bitter

sour

sweet

sour

sweet and salt

1 What are taste buds?
2 Where are taste buds found?
3 List the four tastes that your taste buds can detect.
4 Explain why food does not taste the same when you have a cold.

detect   taste buds

3.3 Come on in – the water is lovely!

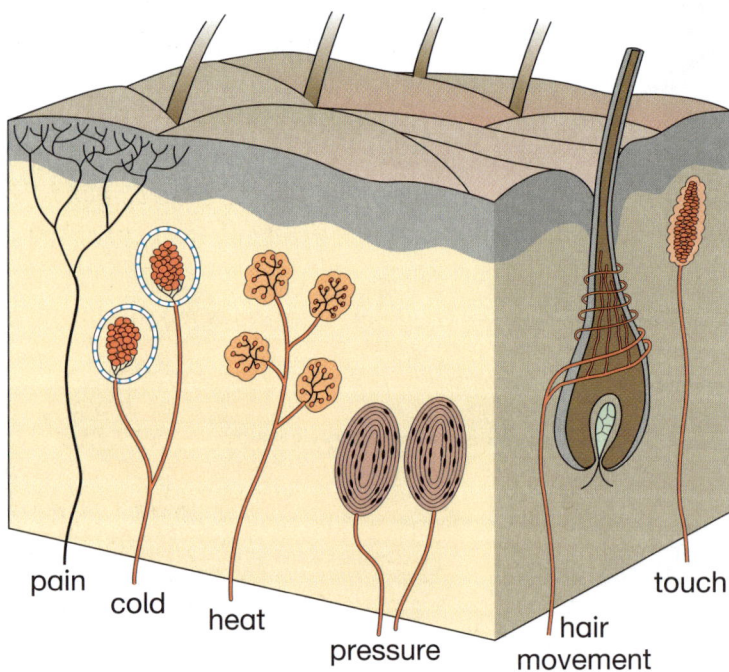

pain cold heat pressure hair movement touch

Would you like to do that? It must be freezing, but these people do it nearly every day and quickly get used to it. The body reacts in many strange ways when it gets cold. We detect cold and heat through our skin.

Skin contains nerves that sense touch, **pressure**, pain and **temperature**. A strong **sensation** is usually felt because lots of nerves have been stimulated. Some parts of your skin are more sensitive than others because there are more nerve endings. Skin cannot detect actual temperature. It detects changes of temperature. That's why warm water can feel cool if you are very hot. Your senses are fooled!

1 Draw and label a diagram of the skin.
2 Name the four stimuli that nerves in the skin can detect.
3 Why do you think pressure sensors are deeper in the skin than touch and pain sensors?
4 Plan an experiment to show how temperature sensors in the skin fool the brain. (Hint: use hot, warm and iced water.)

| pressure | temperature | sensation |

3.4 Optical illusions

3-D vision is something we take for granted. 3-D means three dimensional. It enables us to judge distances. We look at something and can tell how far away it is without thinking. Photographs and computer displays still cannot give us realistic 3-D pictures.

Each one of our eyes sees a slightly different view of the world around us. The brain combines the two images so we see in 3-D. The Victorians used photographs taken from slightly different positions to achieve the **illusion** of 3-D vision.

You can prove that 3-D, or **stereoscopic**, vision helps us to judge distances. Hold a pencil in your right hand. Shut your right eye and hold your right arm straight in front of you. Try to touch the tip of the pencil with your left hand. Could you do it? Now try with both eyes open.

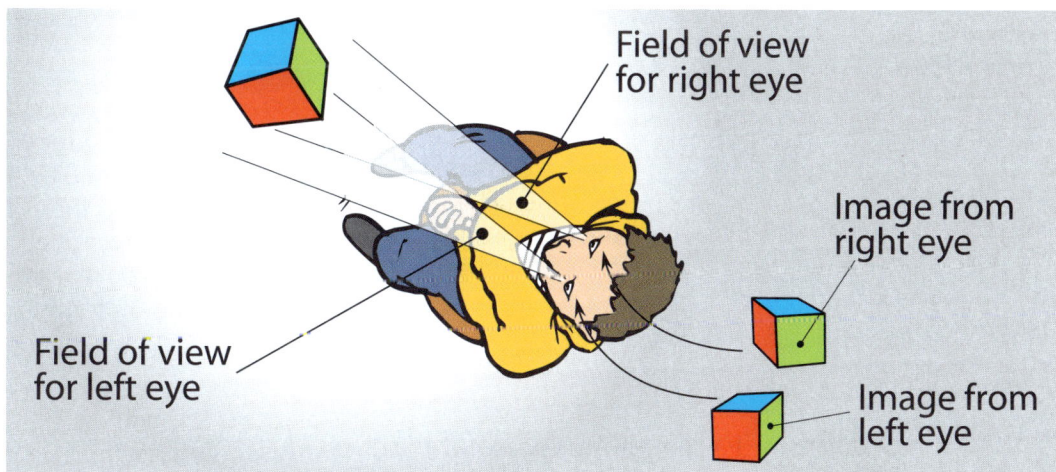

Field of view for right eye

Image from right eye

Field of view for left eye

Image from left eye

1 What does 3-D mean?
2 What does 3-D vision enable us to do?
3 Explain how we can see in 3-D.

| 3-D | illusion | stereoscopic |

4

4.1 Really useful plants!

Plants are very useful in our everyday lives. We eat them, sit on them, use them to dye our clothes and take them as medicines.

Some plant materials do not have to be changed very much before we can use them. Wood only needs to be cut and preserved and dyes can be collected by **grinding** up the plant. Other materials have to be **extracted** from the plant. Crushing seeds removes most of the oil but the rest must be taken out **chemically**. Medicines are often extracted chemically too and many perfumes can be collected by **distillation**.

Steam rises and goes into the delivery tube.

Steam passes over the orange peel. The orange oil evaporates.

The ice cools the orange vapour. Drops of oil form on the delivery tube and collect at the bottom.

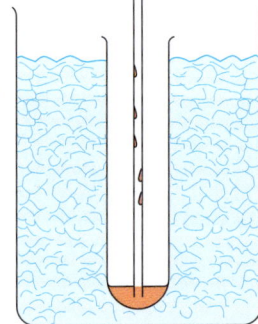

1 List as many useful plant products as you can. Try to get at least 10.
2 Sort your list into products for homes, clothing, cosmetics and toiletries, and medicine.
3 List four seeds used to make oil.
4 Describe a simple way to collect the perfume from rose petals.

| grinding | extract | chemically | distillation |

4.2 Making a meal of plants

Many plants provide animals with **nutrients** such as carbohydrates, fats, proteins, vitamins and minerals. Other plants just add flavour. For example, there is very little nutritional value in many spices – but a curry without spices wouldn't be very tasty!

Every part of a plant has a function. Two very important parts are the **leaves** and the **roots**. The leaves of a plant make food. They do this by **photosynthesis**. The roots **anchor** the plant in the soil. They also take in water and minerals.

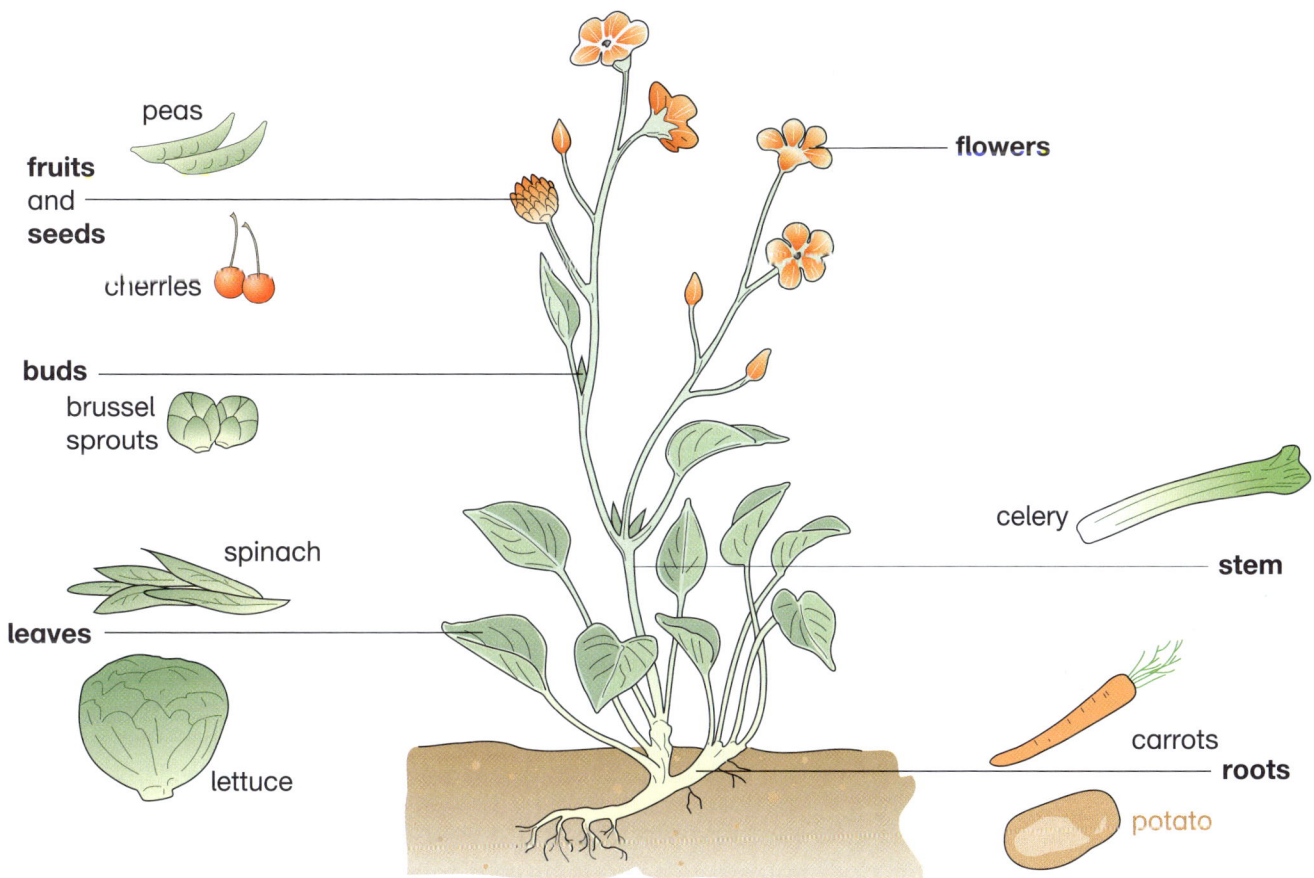

peas

fruits and seeds

cherries

buds

brussel sprouts

spinach

leaves

lettuce

flowers

celery

stem

carrots

roots

potato

1 Use the drawing above to list all the parts of a plant.
2 Explain what the leaves do.
3 Explain what the roots do.
4 Plan an investigation to see if small grapes are sweeter than large grapes.

nutrients   leaves   roots   photosynthesis   anchor
buds   seeds   fruit   flower   stem

4.3 Growing seeds

This huge great tree has grown from a tiny seed! But what would happen if lots of these giant trees grew close together? Seeds must be carried away from their parents to find room to grow. This is called **dispersal**. Dispersal makes sure that seedlings do not grow too close to their parent and so compete for light, water, space and nutrients.

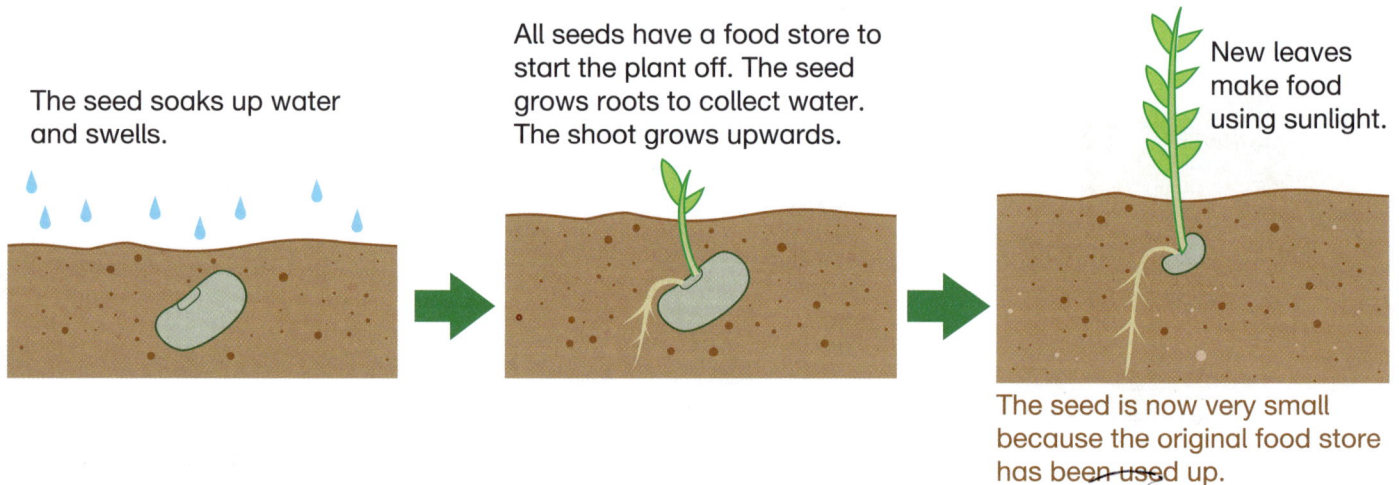

The seed soaks up water and swells.

All seeds have a food store to start the plant off. The seed grows roots to collect water. The shoot grows upwards.

New leaves make food using sunlight.

The seed is now very small because the original food store has been used up.

Seeds only grow into new plants if the conditions are right. They need water, air and warmth. All seeds have a food store to start the plant off. The seed must grow **roots** to collect water, and **leaves** to make more food before the food store runs out. This early growth is called **germination**.

1 Why do plants make seeds?
2 Why must the seeds be dispersed?
3 What three things do seeds need to help them germinate?
4 Which part of the seed grows first?
5 What is it used for?

| dispersal | roots | leaves | germination |

4.4　More than just mud!

Mud is complicated stuff! And good garden soil is even more complicated! When seeds reach a patch of bare soil they need a lot of things to be able to grow properly.

Soil gives protective cover to bulbs and seeds and provides darkness for germination. It also provides minerals and nutrients, air and water to growing plants. It is the place where many **micro-organisms** such as bacteria and **fungi** live. Many larger organisms such as earthworms also live in soil.

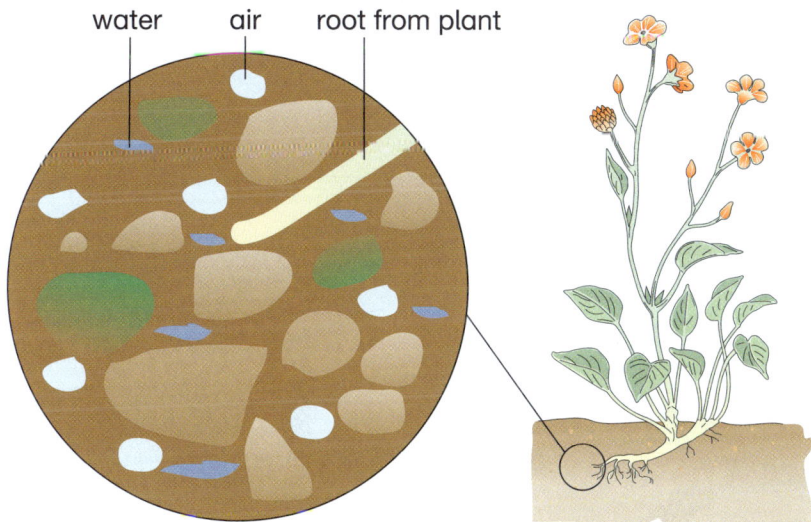

Soil is made from rock fragments and humus. **Humus** is the decayed remains of plants and animals. These decayed remains are sticky and hold the soil together.

water　air　root from plant

There are different types of soil and this affects the type of plant that will grow in it. Dry sandy soils, like those found in **deserts**, have specially adapted plants such as cacti. **Waterlogged** soils, found in **estuaries** and **swampy** places, will have more aquatic plants growing there. Soils with a lot of **clay** in them will often become waterlogged. Gardeners like good **loam** soils for growing vegetables and flowers.

1　List three things the soil gives to growing seeds.
2　What is soil made from?
3　List the different types of soil.
4　How does the type of soil affect the type of plant that grows there?

| soil | micro-organism | fungi | humus | desert |
| waterlogged | estuary | swamp | clay | loam |

5.1 Algae

This woman is drying **seaweed** in the sun to be used in cooking. In Wales a different kind of seaweed is used to make a food called laverbread. Seaweeds belong to a group of living things called **algae**, which grow in seas all around the world. They are useful as a food because they contain lots of minerals. Substances made from algae can also be used as medicines or to thicken food.

ice creams

toothpaste

Smile

fresh

medicines

seaweed

marshmallows

agar jelly for growing microbes

paper and fabrics

cosmetics

Some algae are **microscopic** plants that live in water. They make ponds and fish tanks look green. These plants carry out **photosynthesis** to make **glucose** and **oxygen**. A large percentage of the oxygen that we breathe is produced by algae.

Carbon dioxide + water + light energy → glucose + oxygen

1 Why is seaweed a useful food?
2 What is agar jelly used for?
3 Why is it useful that algae produce oxygen?
4 Write out a word equation to show photosynthesis.

seaweed	algae	agar	microscopic
photosynthesis	glucose	oxygen	

5.2 Fungi

Mushrooms are large **fungi** that we can eat. Fungi are a group of living things that cannot make their own food. They live on food that has been produced by something else. The mushrooms that you eat probably grew on horse manure!

Fungi are used to make **antibiotics** such as **penicillin**. Blue cheeses such as Stilton and Danish Blue have very tiny fungi added to them to give them flavour. In Japan, fungi are used in the manufacture of Sake, a wine made from rice.

This orange has gone mouldy. It has been invaded by microscopic fungi. **Mould** is another name for microscopic fungi. Mould will live wherever there is warmth, food and moisture. That's why clothes can go mouldy if they are put away damp. Microscopic fungi are too small to be seen on their own, but when they multiply into thousands we can see them easily.

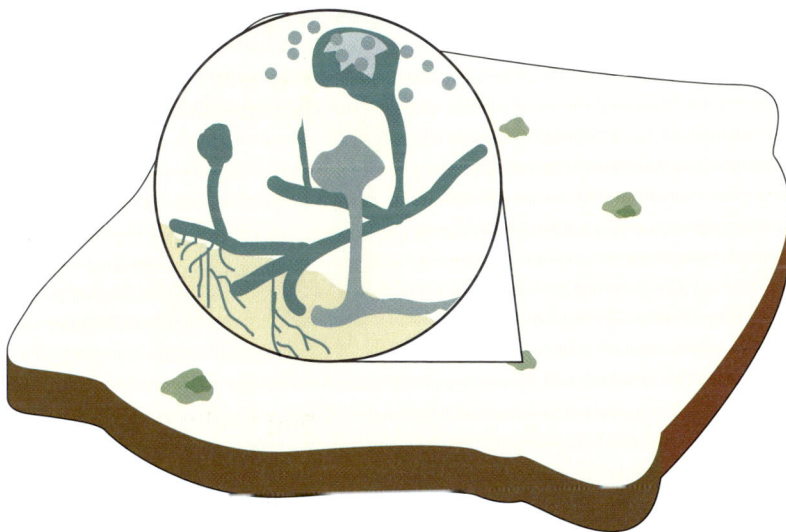

| Spore lands on food in a warm, moist place. |
| Spore grows to produce a mat of fungal threads over the food. |
| After a while the threads produce their own spores to spread to new places. |
| Spores travel in the air to new food sources. |

1 Can fungi make their own food like other plants?
2 Make two columns. At the top of one column write the heading 'How fungi can be helpful'. At the top of the other column write the heading 'How fungi can be harmful'. Put at least three examples in each column.
3 What things do fungi need to survive?

fungi   antibiotics   penicillin   mould

5.3 Yeast

These people are crushing grapes with their feet. They are going to make wine. The skins of the fruit contain tiny single-celled fungi called **yeast**. The yeast feeds on the **sugars** in the fruit and changes it to **alcohol**. This is called **fermentation**.

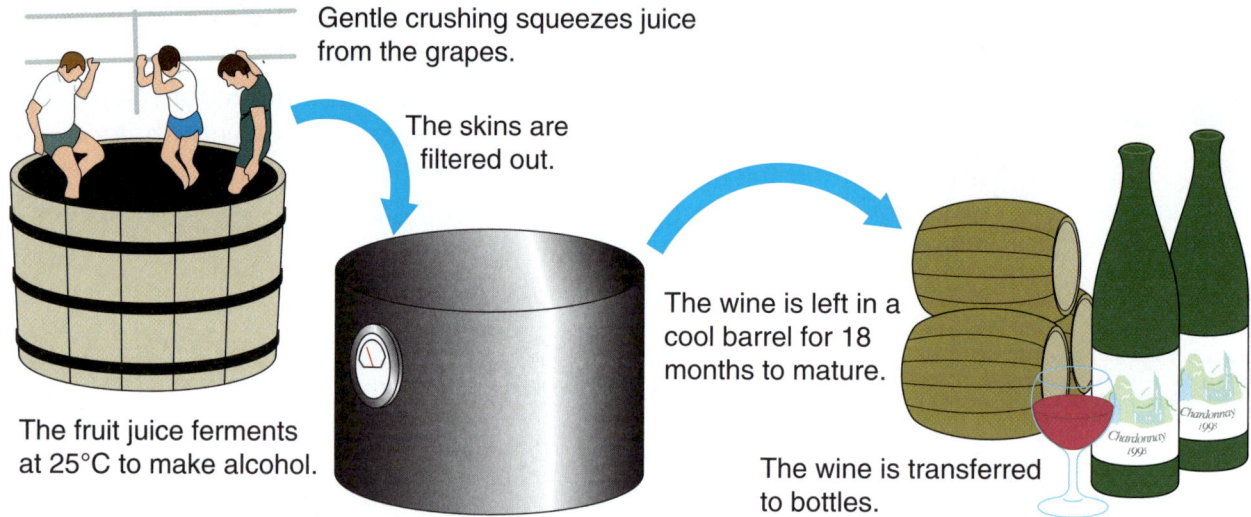

Gentle crushing squeezes juice from the grapes.

The skins are filtered out.

The fruit juice ferments at 25°C to make alcohol.

The wine is left in a cool barrel for 18 months to mature.

The wine is transferred to bottles.

Almost any fruit or vegetable can be used to make wine. Beer is made from barley or wheat instead of fruit. Brewers add hops to give the beer a special flavour. Yeast is made as a **by-product** of **brewing**. Yeast is rich in vitamins and is used in savoury spreads. During fermentation, the yeasts ferment the sugars to produce alcohol and **carbon dioxide**. It is the carbon dioxide that puts the bubbles into beer, wine and champagne.

glucose → alcohol + carbon dioxide + energy

Fermentation is also used in baking and to make antibiotics. When the yeast in bread dough is warm, moist and has sugar to feed on, it ferments. The carbon dioxide produced makes the dough rise and the bubbles trapped in the dough make the bread light. The alcohol produced by fermentation evaporates when the dough is cooked.

1 What two things does yeast produce when fermenting sugar?
2 What conditions does yeast need to ferment?
3 Why are savoury spreads made from yeast good for you?
4 Draw a flow chart to show the main stages in making wine.

yeast	sugar	alcohol	fermentation
by-product	brewing	carbon dioxide	

5.4 Bacteria

Edam cheese has a red waxy coating to stop it drying out. You're not supposed to eat the coating – but it probably won't do you much harm! It's important to store cheese in good conditions or it will dry out or go mouldy. Even the **bacteria** used to make the cheese in the first place could make it go off.

Bacteria need moisture, warmth and a food supply before they can grow. If special bacteria, called **lactic acid bacteria**, are added to milk which is kept warm, they feed on the milk and multiply, turning it into **yoghurt**.

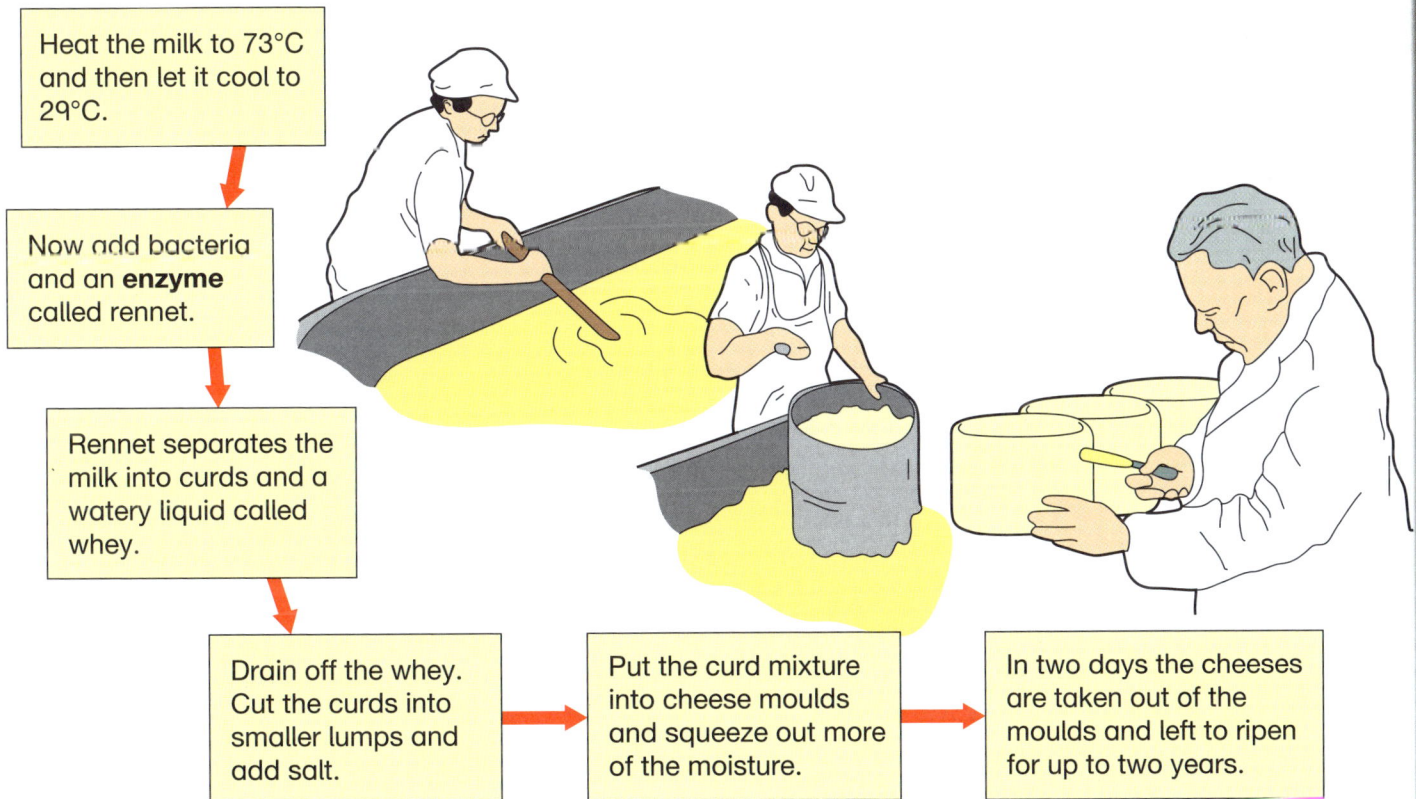

Heat the milk to 73°C and then let it cool to 29°C.

Now add bacteria and an **enzyme** called rennet.

Rennet separates the milk into curds and a watery liquid called whey.

Drain off the whey. Cut the curds into smaller lumps and add salt.

Put the curd mixture into cheese moulds and squeeze out more of the moisture.

In two days the cheeses are taken out of the moulds and left to ripen for up to two years.

1 Why is it important to store cheese in the correct conditions?
2 Why is the enzyme rennet added to the milk in the cheese-making process?
3 Name three things that bacteria need to grow.
4 Plan an investigation to see how temperature affects how quickly milk turns sour.

| bacteria | lactic acid bacteria | yoghurt | enzyme |

6.1 Stranding around!

Leeloo is the supreme being who saves the world in the film *The Fifth Element*. She may look human, but her genes are very different from ours! **Genes** are small lengths of a chemical called **DNA**, found in our cells. They provide the instructions the body needs to make things. So, if you have brown eyes it is because you contain a gene that tells your body how to make brown eyes.

Chromosomes are long strings of genes stuck together. They are found in the **nucleus** of cells. A chromosome contains hundreds of thousands of genes. Individual genes are far too small to see even with the most powerful microscope. Chromosomes can be seen with a microscope that can magnify objects up to 1000 times.

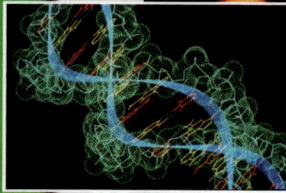

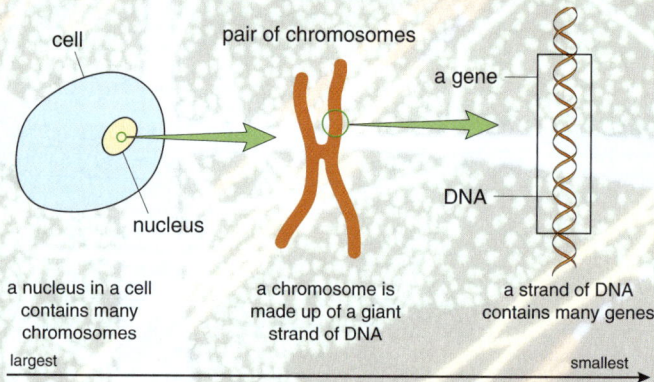

cell · pair of chromosomes · a gene · nucleus · DNA

a nucleus in a cell contains many chromosomes — largest

a chromosome is made up of a giant strand of DNA

a strand of DNA contains many genes — smallest

So why is Leeloo so different from us? Our DNA has two strands that twine around each other. Leeloo's DNA has many strands, but they still carry genes.

Humans have 46 chromosomes. 44 of these are arranged into 22 pairs. The last, or 23rd, pair are the sex chromosomes, which decide if we are male or female. There are two types of sex chromosome, one called the **X chromosome**, and a slightly shorter one called the **Y chromosome**. Women have two X chromosomes. Men have one X and one Y chromosome.

1 Write a sentence containing the word gene.
2 Rank these structures by size, starting with the smallest.
   chromosome   gene   cell   nucleus
3 What is a chromosome?
4 What is the difference between the sex chromosomes in women and the sex chromosomes in men?

gene   DNA   chromosomes   nucleus
X chromosome   Y chromosome

My genes

24

6.2 Like father, like son?

Your parents passed their genes on to you. So are you like them? Well, yes and no. You will have **inherited** some of your parents characteristics, but the **environment** will also affect how you look.

Just like chromosomes, genes come in pairs. Half of your genes will have come from your mum and half from your dad. If your mum and dad both gave you the same genes, for example genes for blue eyes, then you will have blue eyes. But what happens if your mum gave you a gene for brown eyes? In this case one of the genes is **dominant** and controls how you look. The other gene is **recessive** and will not have any affect. The gene for brown eyes is dominant to the gene for blue eyes. So you end up with brown eyes.

Punnett square

Genes from mum

Genes from dad

	B	B
b	Bb	Bb
b	Bb	Bb

Parents	Offspring
Brown × Blue BB × bb	All offspring will have brown eyes Bb

Another reason that you may not look exactly like your parents is because your environment is different to theirs. Imagine that you fell over when you were young and cut your forehead. The cut will have healed but you may have a scar for the rest of your life. Neither of your parents will have this scar. These sorts of differences are due to the environment.

1 Write a sentence using the words gene and dominant.
2 Is the gene for blue eyes recessive or dominant to brown eyes?
3 Half of your genes come from your father, where do the other half come from?

inherited   environment   dominant   recessive

6.3 Gene therapy

In the future we may be able to decide which genes our children get. We may be able to ask for blue eyes, or fair hair, or even the chance to be good at music. But what happens if something goes wrong, or if your parents could not afford the expensive genetic treatments?

The way you look is not the only thing you can inherit from your parents. You can also inherit diseases. Diseases such as **cystic fibrosis**, **haemophilia** and **colour deficiency** are caused by mistakes in the genes. If your parents have these genes and pass them on to you, you will inherit the disease.

Today, **genetic engineers** can insert particular genes into cells. This allows them to control how the cell develops. Cystic fibrosis is caused by a mistake in just one gene. People with cystic fibrosis suffer from lots of lung infections and find it difficult to digest their food. Genetic engineers know which gene causes the problem. They are trying to find a way to insert a new, healthy gene into cells in the lungs and cure the disease.

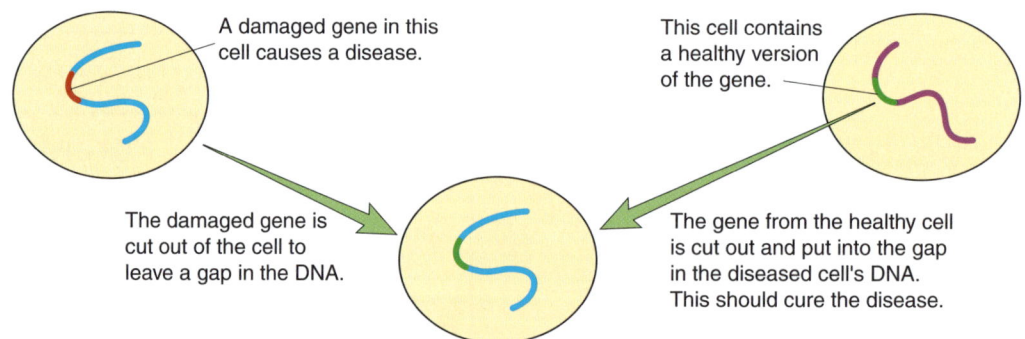

A damaged gene in this cell causes a disease.

This cell contains a healthy version of the gene.

The damaged gene is cut out of the cell to leave a gap in the DNA.

The gene from the healthy cell is cut out and put into the gap in the diseased cell's DNA. This should cure the disease.

Genetic engineering is very difficult. **Selective breeding** of plants and animals is much easier. People have been doing this for hundreds of years. Farmers would select the best cows and bulls to produce calves. Over many generations the calves would be bred to be bigger, or to produce more milk. It is possible to do the same thing with plants. All the different types of apple come from one original apple. Over hundreds of years all the different apples that now exist have been produced by picking the best trees and **crossbreeding** them with other good trees. Selective breeding is also used to make plants resistant to diseases.

1 What is cystic fibrosis?
2 How are genetic engineers trying to cure cystic fibrosis?
3 What do farmers use selective breeding for?

| cystic fibrosis | haemophilia | colour deficiency |
| genetic engineering | selective breeding | crossbreeding |

6.4 Clone attack

Clones are **organisms** with the same genes. Take a potato and plant it. When it grows it will produce a plant that will give you lots of new potatoes. Plant these potatoes and all of the plants that grow will be clones of the first one.

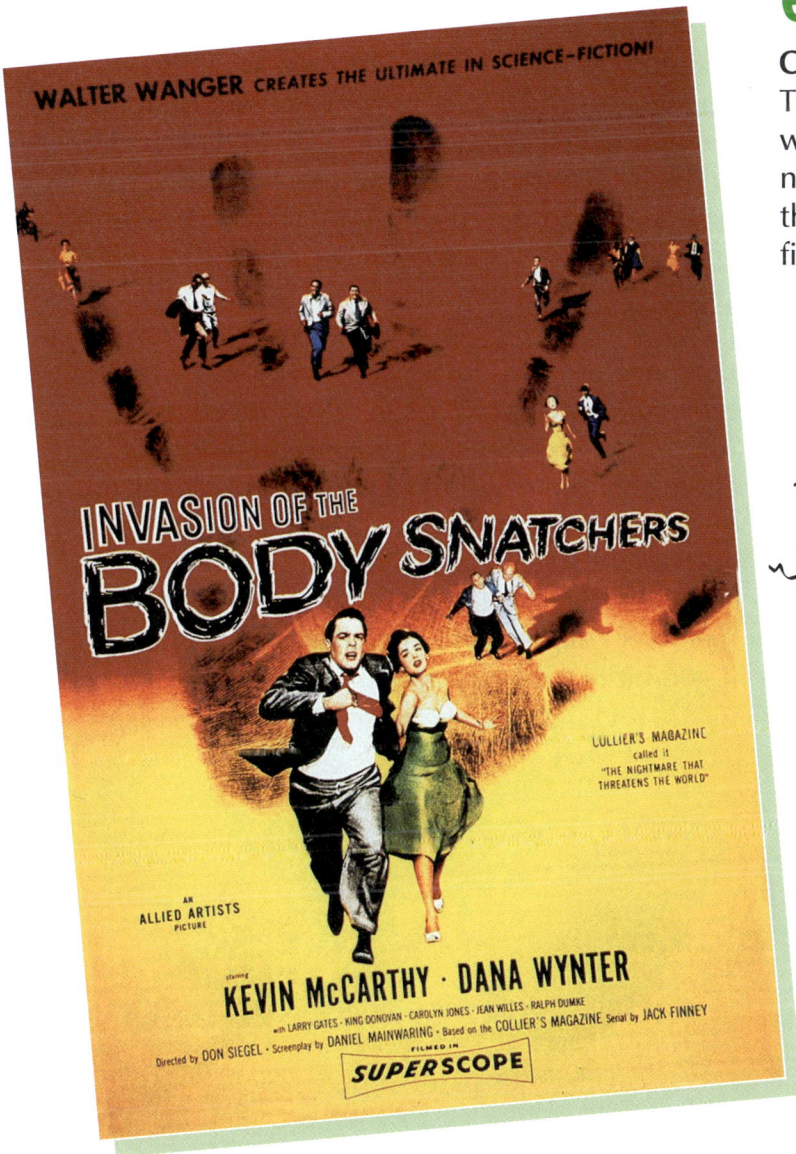

Garden centres often clone plants. Because cloned plants all have the same genes, they behave in the same way. They flower and fruit at the same time, which makes harvesting them easier. It is often quicker and cheaper to clone plants rather than wait for them to grow from seeds. **Cuttings** of roses produce clones in a single season; growing roses from seeds takes much longer.

Unfortunately, as cloned plants are all **identical**, they will all suffer from the same diseases. This means a farmer could lose an entire crop in one go if a pest gets into the field.

1 What does the word clone mean?
2 Give two examples of cloned plants.
3 Give two advantages of cloning plants.
4 Give a disadvantage of cloning plants.

| clone | organism | cutting | identical |

7.1 Eternal youth in a cream?

Everyone wants to look younger! Millions of pounds are spent every year to colour grey hair. Some people even have a facelift to pull the skin on their face tighter so that it looks younger. If you can't afford a facelift how about a cream with special **enzymes** to firm up your skin? But does it work?

Enzymes are very large, complicated molecules made of **protein**. They speed up reactions in the body by linking together the chemicals that need to react. The chemicals are held together in the correct positions so that they can react more easily. There are lots of different enzymes. Each one has a specific shape, which means it can only link together certain chemicals. It is a bit like a key fitting a lock.

Lock and key model

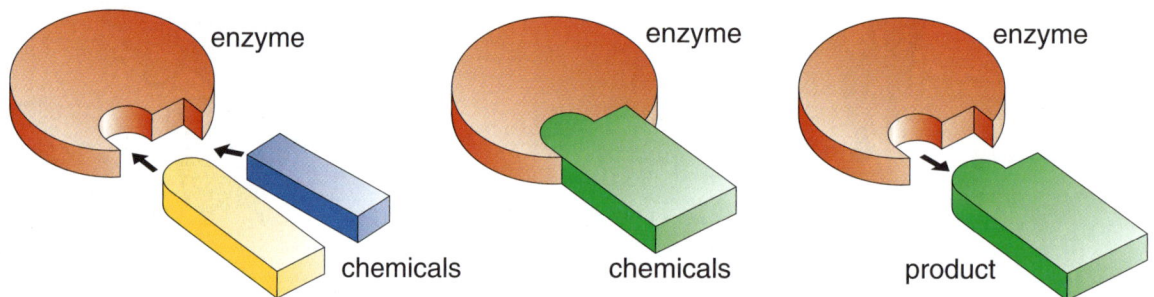

Our gut depends on enzymes to digest food. They break down large food molecules like **starch** and protein into smaller molecules, which can pass into the body. In the body, different enzymes will join the small molecules together to build or repair body parts.

But can enzymes keep us looking younger? Unfortunately, they are such large molecules that they probably can't pass through our skin. So, you're better off saving your money. You never know, you may need a facelift one day!

1 What is an enzyme?
2 What is the lock and key model?
3 What does our gut use enzymes for?
4 Why would a cream containing enzymes not make us look younger?

| enzyme | protein | lock and key model | starch |

7.2 Breaking down

When we die, **enzymes** in the gut keep working, breaking down any food. This helps the police to work out how long ago a dead person last ate. If the food has been completely digested, the last meal was a long time ago. If there is still plenty of undigested food in the gut, the meal was recent.

During digestion, enzymes break down large food molecules into smaller ones. Different enzymes act on different types of food. This helps the police to work out what someone ate for their last meal from the remains in their gut.

Enzyme	Made by	Works in	Acts on	To make
Amylase	Salivary glands	Mouth	Starch	Sugars
Protease	Stomach lining	Stomach	Protein	Amino acids
Lipase	Pancreas	Small intestine	Fats	Fatty acids

The temperature of the body affects how quickly digestion occurs. Enzymes work best at 37°C – normal body temperature. Cooler temperatures slow down enzyme reactions. If the temperature is too high, the enzyme is damaged and stops working.

The speed of digestion is also affected by pH. Most enzymes work best at a **neutral** pH, around pH7, but this isn't always true. The pH in our stomach is very acidic, about 2. This is because our stomach contains a lot of acid. The acid helps to break down the food molecules and kills any microbes in the food. The protease enzyme that works in our stomach works best at pH2.

1   What enzyme digests fat?
2   Which food molecules produce sugar when they break down?
3   How would putting a dead body in a freezer affect how quickly the enzymes worked?
4   A dead person's stomach contains very little protein. A witness said they saw the person eating a ham sandwich just before they were knocked over by a car. Why would you be suspicious?

| enzyme | amylase | protease | lipase | neutral |

7.3 Killer bug

Droplets from the air
Cold and flu viruses are carried in tiny droplets of liquid from people's mouths and noses. They enter your body when you breathe them in.

Contaminated water
Cholera bacteria and polio viruses are transmitted in water. Water can be contaminated if it comes into contact with untreated human sewage. The bacteria and viruses can enter your body if you swim in the water or swallow it.

Contaminated food
Food-poisoning bacteria can be passed out of people's bodies in their faeces. The problem is often caused by preparing food with dirty hands (that may look clean but perhaps have not been washed properly).

Cuts
Tetanus bacteria live in the soil. They can enter your body through a cut.

Bites from animals
The rabies virus lives in the saliva of infected animals such as dogs. It can enter your body through bites.

SARS (Severe Acute Respiratory Syndrome) is a disease that is spread in the same way as normal flu. It produces a very high temperature, a dry cough, difficulty in breathing, headaches and general muscle pain. Fit, young people usually survive SARS but it often kills the old or unfit.

Our skin is a very good barrier that stops **microbes** from getting into our body. Unless you cut yourself, microbes cannot get through it. Even if you do cut yourself, your blood clots quickly to close the cut.

Once a microbe gets into the body, **white blood cells** take over the defence. They protect us in two ways. Some white blood cells produce **antibodies**. Antibodies are chemicals which attack invaders. There is a different antibody for each microbe. Other white blood cells can **engulf** whole microbes. These cells can attack almost any sort of microbe.

1 What does SARS stand for?
2 Why is SARS so dangerous?
3 Which part of the body does SARS affect?
4 How does our skin protect us from attack by microbes?
5 What are the two ways that white blood cells protect the body?

| SARS | microbe | white blood cells | antibody | engulf |

7.4 The Pill

The Pill is a blessing. It gives women more control over their bodies. It means they don't have to rely on men for contraception. It has prevented many unwanted pregnancies and made for happier, smaller families.

The Pill is a terrible thing. It encourages people to sleep around because they think it's safe – they can't get pregnant. But there are other dangers. Sexual infections like syphilis and AIDS, the breakdown of relationships and rising divorce rates are all linked to the Pill. It would be better if it had never been discovered.

Strong views. But what do you think? And how does the Pill work anyway? The Pill depends on chemicals called **hormones**. Hormones are natural chemicals produced by glands in the body. These glands secrete the hormones into the bloodstream.

The two female sex hormones, **oestrogen** and **progesterone**, are made in the **ovaries**. These hormones are very important as they control **ovulation** and the **menstrual cycle**. Once a month the ovaries release an egg. If the egg is fertilised, the ovaries produce more oestrogen and progesterone. This stops any more eggs being released. If the egg is not fertilised, the levels of oestrogen and progesterone fall and after about 21 days the ovaries release another egg.

The Pill keeps the levels of oestrogen and progesterone high. This makes the body think it is pregnant and no eggs are released.

Changing the levels of the sex hormones in a woman's blood is not only used to prevent pregnancy. Doctors also use these hormones in **fertility treatment**, encouraging the ovaries to release an egg.

1 Write a sentence using the word hormone.
2 What part of the body makes the hormones progesterone and oestrogen?
3 What does progesterone do to the body?

hormones	oestrogen	progesterone	ovary
ovulation	menstrual cycle	fertility treatment	

Strong stuff

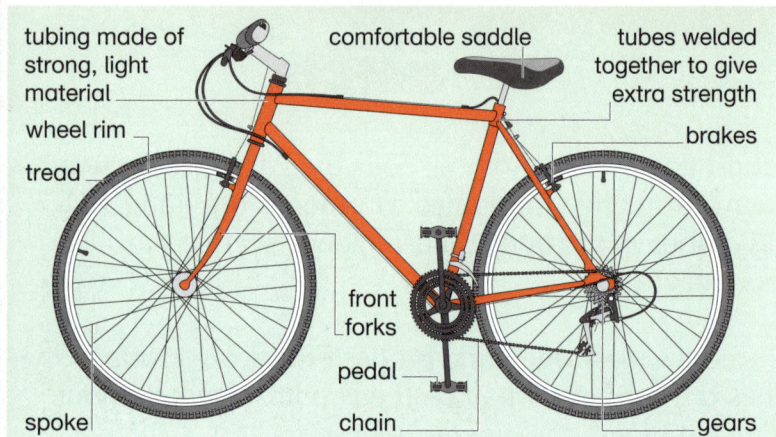

8.1 On your bike!

The materials used to make a bike can be sorted into two groups – **metals** and **non-metals**. These two groups have different properties. Metals are usually stronger. They can also **conduct** heat and electricity better than non-metals like plastics and rubber.

In the past, metals were the strongest, lightest materials you could use to make mountain bikes. These days, materials developed in chemistry laboratories are at least as strong as metals and are often lighter and cheaper to make.

The frame of the mountain bike shown in the photograph is made of an alloy. **Alloys** are mixtures of two or more metals. The properties of an alloy may be very different from the properties of the pure metals it contains.

Metal or alloy	Density /g per cm³	Strength (1 = weakest)	Does it rust?
Pure iron	7.9	4	Yes
Pure **aluminium**	2.7	1	No
Aluminium alloy	2.8	8	No
Steel alloy	2.8	6	Yes
Chromaloy	7.9	9	No

1 List three properties of a metal.
2 What is an alloy?
3 Which of the materials in the table has the lowest **density**?
4 Aluminium alloy bike frames need much thicker tubing than chromaloy ones. Why?
5 Steel frames have to be painted but aluminium alloy frames do not. Why?

| metal | non-metal | conduct | alloy | aluminium |
| density | | | | |

8.2 Joining up

Metal structures usually contain more than one part. To join these parts together the builders can use bolts, or they can **solder** or **weld** the metal pieces. The Eden Project uses thousands of special bolts, each about 15 cm long, to hold the domes together.

If the joint between two metal parts needs to be strong, they are welded together. A soldered joint is less strong. Solder is an alloy of **lead** and **tin** that melts at a low temperature. An electrician often uses solder to join metal wires to a circuit board.

Welding	Soldering	Bolts
Parts get very hot	Parts get hot	Parts do not get hot
The metal melts	Only the solder melts	The nut and bolt hold the parts together
Very strong joint	Weak joint	Joint is as strong as the bolt
Needs heavy welding equipment and gas bottles	Needs a small electric tool	Needs a spanner

In a welded joint the two metals are heated until they melt together.

In a soldered joint the metals do not melt. They are held together by the solder when it goes solid.

1 List four ways to join metal parts together.
2 Builders could not weld parts of the Eden Project domes together. Why?
3 What happens when a joint is welded?
4 Name the two metals solder contains.
5 Why are joints on electrical circuit boards soldered not welded?

solder   weld   lead   tin

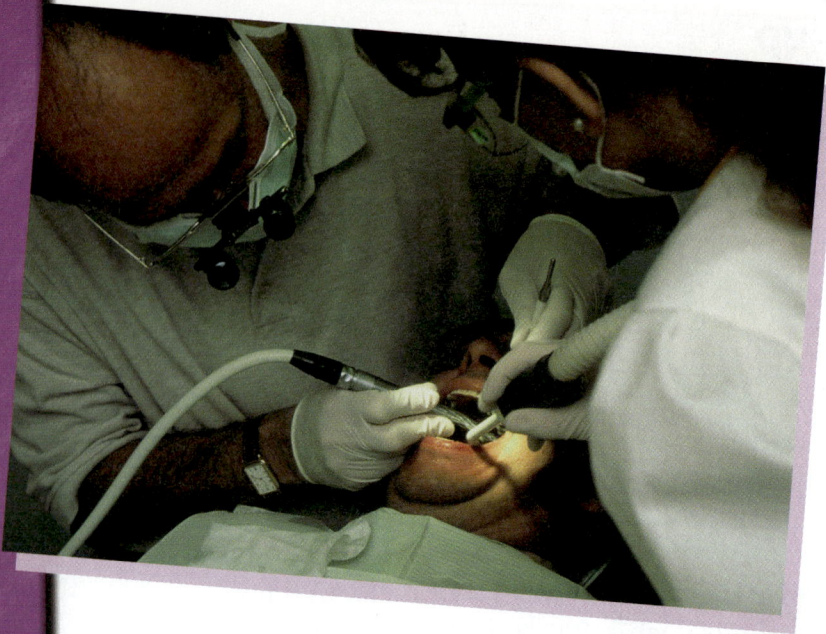

8.3 Filling a gap!

Teeth are made of the hardest substance in the human body. It is called **enamel**. Look after your teeth and they will last a lifetime. But we eat too many sugary foods and that leads to decay. Dentists drill out the decayed part of the tooth and fill the gap with an **alloy**. Sometimes the complete tooth needs to be replaced. Dentists use special plastics or even gold to do this.

Dentists usually use an alloy containing **mercury** to fill teeth. Alloys containing mercury are called **amalgams**. The dentist's assistant mixes silver, copper and other metals with mercury to make a paste. The dentist fills the hole in the tooth with the paste and waits for it to set hard.

Some new fillings use materials called **composites**. A composite is a material that contains two or more different substances. The composite used for fillings contains silica powder and a resin. The resin acts like a glue and sets to make a tough filling.

Mercury amalgam	Silica-resin composite
Silver-grey colour	Can be matched to the colour of the tooth
Contains mercury which is harmful	Contains no mercury
Can produce allergies	No known allergies
Filling has to be wedged into the hole	Filling is bonded to the remains of the tooth
Can be used for filling large holes in back teeth	No good for large holes
Quick to do	Slower to do
Cheaper than composite materials	More expensive than mercury amalgam

1   What name is given to a mixture of metals containing mercury?
2   Write down three advantages of new composite materials for filling teeth.
3   Write down three disadvantages of new composite materials for filling teeth.
4   Plan a test to find out how easily a material for filling teeth can be broken. If you can, carry out your test on samples of plaster or concrete.

| enamel | alloy | mercury | amalgam | composite |

8.4 It's a racket

Tennis players can now hit a ball so hard that it travels at over 100 mph! Get in the way of one of those serves and you could get something worse than a black eye! The top speed of a tennis serve has been going up over the last few years. Is this because the players are getting stronger or is it something to do with the tennis rackets?

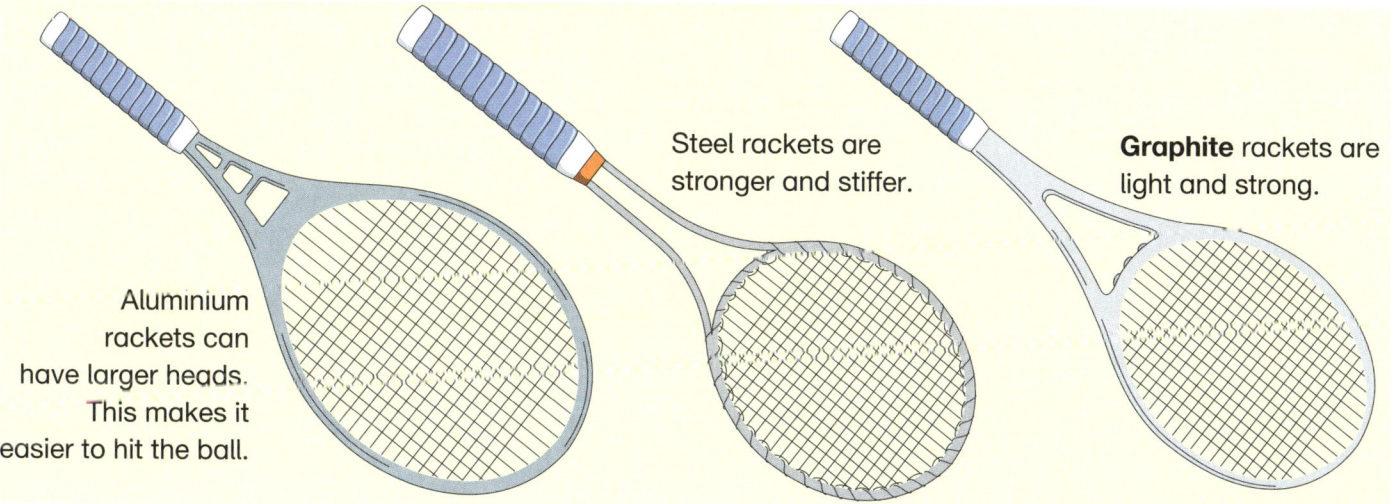

Aluminium rackets can have larger heads. This makes it easier to hit the ball.

Steel rackets are stronger and stiffer.

Graphite rackets are light and strong.

Material	Density /g cm³	Strength (1 = weakest)	Does it rust?
Wood	0.7	3	No
Aluminium alloy	2.8	8	No
Steel	7.8	6	Yes
Graphite	1.9	15	No
Rubber	0.9	0.2	No
Polythene	0.9	0.1	No

1 Which material is the strongest?
2 Give two advantages of using graphite over steel to make a tennis racket.
3 Draw a bar chart to show the differences in strength of the materials in the table.
4 Tight strings on a racket give a firmer surface for the ball to hit. Does this give a stronger serve? Plan an investigation to find out how the surface a ball bounces on affects the height of the bounce.

graphite   density

9.1 Sediments

Not the safest sport ever! Does it even look like fun? Yet all over the country people spend time in dark, wet caves!

The best caves are found in **limestone** rocks. Limestone is a **sedimentary** rock. It is formed by water from the remains of tiny creatures or from chemical deposits. These are pressed together to form solid rock.

There are lots of other sorts of sedimentary rock. These include **sandstone** and **mudstone**. They are all formed in layers from small particles. It can take millions of years to make a metre of sedimentary rock.

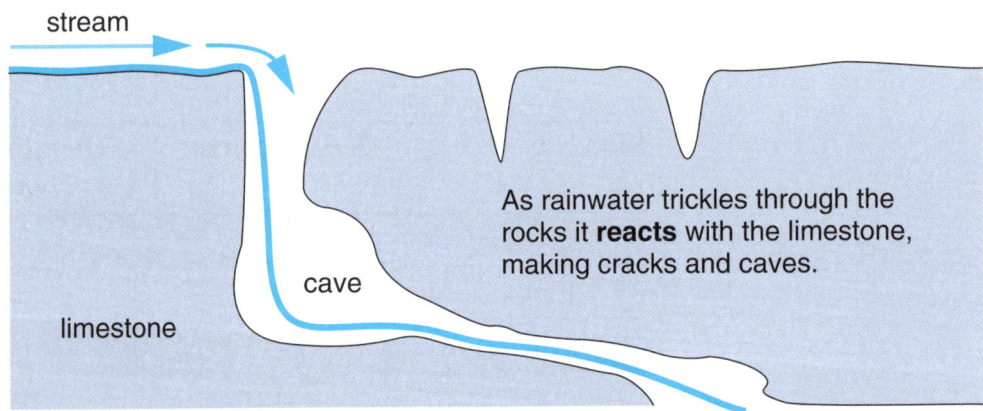

stream

limestone

cave

As rainwater trickles through the rocks it **reacts** with the limestone, making cracks and caves.

Limestone is often used for statues and buildings. This is because it is easily available, easy to work and looks attractive. Unfortunately, limestone can be eroded by heat and cold. Acid rain also affects limestone, speeding up the erosion and making the rock crumble.

1 Name two types of sedimentary rock.
2 Explain how sedimentary rocks are formed.
3 Why is limestone often used for building work?
4 What is the problem with using limestone for statues and buildings?
5 Explain, using diagrams, how rainwater makes caves.

| limestone | sedimentary | sandstone | mudstone |
| react | | | |

9.2 Minerals and crystals

Diamonds are forever – but finding them involves a huge amount of dangerous and dirty work. Diamonds are expensive because they are rare and beautiful. They are formed deep in the Earth where it is very hot and the rocks are under great **pressure**.

A **mineral** is any chemical found in a rock. So a rock is a mixture of different minerals. Different minerals form **crystals** that have different shapes and colours. You can grow crystals yourself by leaving mineral **solutions** in a warm place. As the water **evaporates** from the solution, the crystals grow. The quicker the water evaporates the smaller the crystals. Some hard minerals are used for making jewellery. Most minerals don't look like crystals at all.

A diamond is a very hard mineral. Most of the valuable minerals which are used for jewellery are very hard. If something is hard it will scratch anything that is less hard than itself. Modern glass cutters use a very hard metal blade to scratch glass. The glass can then be snapped cleanly along the scratch. In the past, a tiny diamond was used instead.

1 What is a mineral?
2 Explain how you could grow some mineral crystals at home.
3 How would you find out whether glass was harder than plastic?
4 Give two reasons why diamonds are so expensive.

| pressure | mineral | crystal | solution | evaporate |
| diamond | | | | |

9.3 Earthquake!

Earthquakes happen when layers of rock move past each other and shake the Earth's surface. Many people have been killed when buildings have collapsed on them. Modern buildings are built from materials that can withstand the force of some earthquakes.

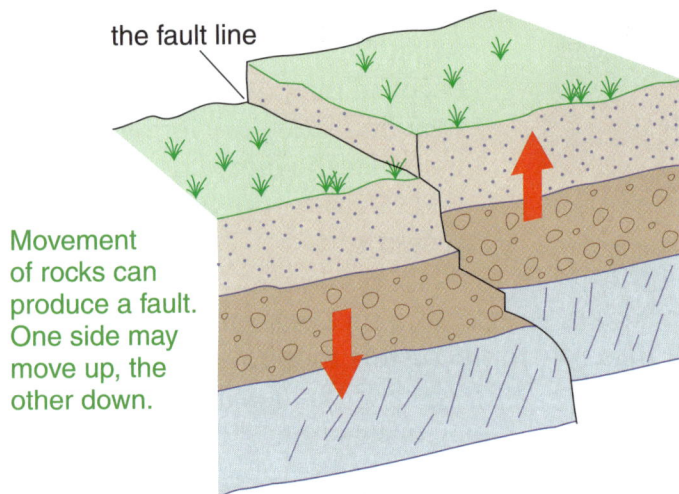

the fault line

Movement of rocks can produce a fault. One side may move up, the other down.

The heat and pressure from the movement of rocks underground can be enormous. This heat and pressure changes the rocks. For example, heat and pressure can change the sedimentary rock limestone into **marble**. Marble is a **metamorphic** rock. Metamorphic rocks are made when heat and pressure act on other rocks.

Buildings can be built from many different materials. In countries where there are plenty of trees, many homes are built from wood. In other places, lots of homes are built with bricks. Bricks are made from **clay** and are joined together with **mortar**. Mortar is made from sand and **cement**.

Concrete is another building material. It is made from sand, cement and small stones. Concrete can be made stronger (**reinforced**) by putting metal rods or glass fibre into it.

1 How do earthquakes happen?
2 How can concrete be reinforced?
3 What is a metamorphic rock?
4 Give one example of a metamorphic rock.

| marble | metamorphic | clay | mortar | cement |
| concrete | reinforced | | | |

9.4 Volcanoes

The inside of the Earth is so hot that rocks melt. A **volcano** is a place on the surface of the Earth where hot, melted rock comes out. Dust, smoke and large lumps of solid rock often **erupt** from volcanoes too. Rocks that come from volcanoes are called **igneous** rocks. Volcanoes may lie **dormant** for many years and then suddenly erupt.

The surface of the Earth is made up of a number of pieces called **plates**. These plates move around at a speed of a few centimetres per year. Earthquakes and volcanoes are common along the edges of plates. They are rare in the middle of plates.

Some liquid rock never reaches the surface. It is called **magma**. It cools slowly and forms rock called **granite** that has large crystals. Granite is often used for building.

The liquid rock flowing along the surface is called **lava**. It cools quite quickly into a dark rock that contains small crystals.

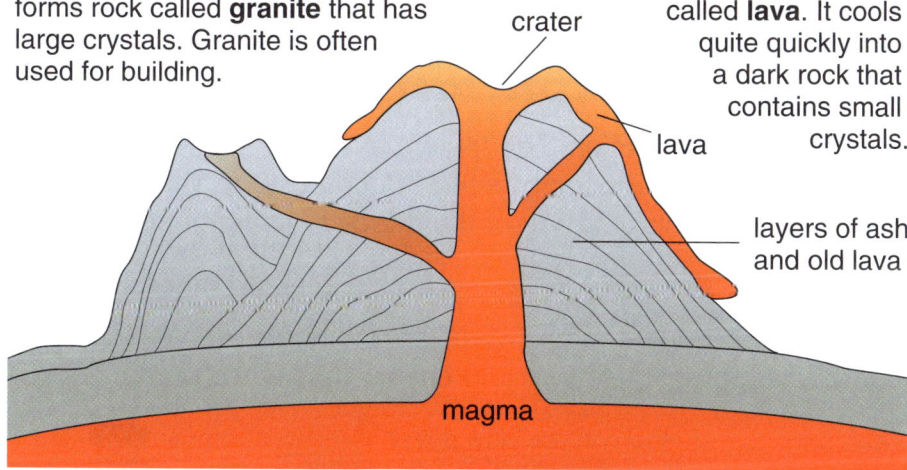

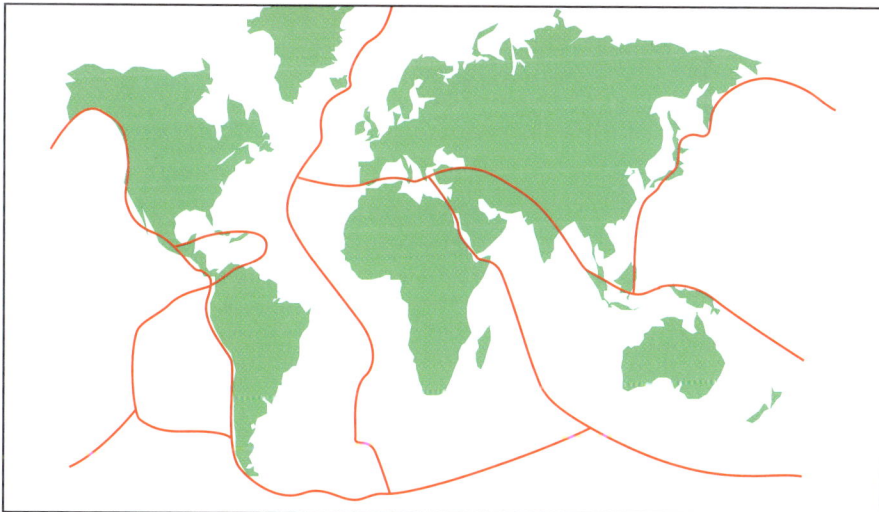

1 What is an igneous rock?
2 Why do some igneous rocks have large crystals in them?
3 What is the difference between magma and lava?
4 Why are there no volcanoes or major earthquakes in Britain?

| volcano | erupt | igneous | dormant | magma |
| granite | lava | plates | | |

10.1 Reactions

A bonfire is a giant **chemical reaction**. The things on the bonfire **react** with oxygen in the air. We call this reaction burning or **combustion**. The faster the reaction the better the bonfire! If any of the things reacting are used up, the reaction stops.

Not all chemical reactions happen at the same speed. Some are very fast, others take a long time. Sometimes we try to change the speed of reactions.

Some gravestones crumble faster than others. What can affect the speed at which gravestones crumble?

How can you slow down the speed at which milk will turn sour?

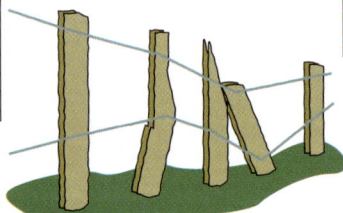

What can you do to slow down the rotting of the fence?

These iron pots are thousands of years old. **Rusting** is a chemical reaction.

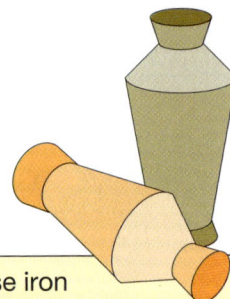

One way to speed up a reaction is to increase the temperature. This gives the reacting chemicals more energy. You can make sugar dissolve in water much more quickly if you increase the temperature of the water.

1   What is the scientific name for the reaction we call burning?
2   How could you make a bonfire burn more brightly?
3   What stops the bonfire burning in the end?
4   List three very fast chemical reactions.
5   List three very slow chemical reactions.

chemical reaction	react	combustion	rust

In the *Alien* films the monster has **acid** for blood. This makes it very difficult to kill. If the monster is injured, it will release acid which will eat its way through the metal hull of the spaceship.

Everyone thinks that acids are very dangerous. However, acids are not always good at dissolving metal. The **reaction** between an acid and a metal can be quite slow.

Steven did a series of experiments with zinc metal and hydrochloric acid. These are his results.

Table 1. The metal is added as a large lump.

Acid	Amount of metal /g	Time to dissolve /secs
Dilute	10	20
Concentrated	10	13

Table 2. The metal is added as a fine powder.

Acid	Amount of metal /g	Time to dissolve /secs
Dilute	10	12
Concentrated	10	5

1 Which conditions dissolved the metal quickest?
2 What was the longest time taken to dissolve 10 g of metal?
3 How did using powder instead of lumps affect the speed of the reaction?
4 List three ways to speed up the reaction between an acid and a metal.

acid   reaction

Skateboards, snowboards and surf boards – they are all made from plastic **resin**. The resin is moulded to the right shape and then sanded to perfection. To make the resin go solid in the mould, a hardener is used. The hardener contains a **catalyst**. The resin does go solid without the hardener but it is a very, very slow **reaction**. The catalyst speeds up the setting time. Other catalysts can speed up different reactions. Changing the **temperature** can affect the rate of the reaction as well.

Hardener in 100 g of the mixture /g	Time for paste to set /mins
10	20
20	14
30	12
40	10
50	10
60	14

Temperature /°C	Time for paste to set /mins
10	30
20	12
30	10
40	6
50	2

1 What affect does heating have on the setting time?
2 What affect does using more hardener in the mixture have on the setting time?
3 Would anything happen to the paste if it was left for ten minutes without mixing with the hardener?
4 It says on the pack that you should not mix more than you can use in ten minutes. Why?

resin	catalyst	reaction	temperature

10.4 Enzymes

Munich has one of the largest beer festivals in the world! In 2002 six million visitors downed millions of litres of beer and maybe just a few headache pills!

Beer, and all other alcoholic drinks, depend on **yeast**. Yeast is a living organism, which uses **catalysts** to speed up reactions. The catalysts in living organisms are called **enzymes**.

Enzymes allow living things to carry out all sorts of reactions at low temperatures. The reactions in yeast produce **alcohol** and **carbon dioxide** from sugar. The enzymes will not work if the temperature is too hot or too cold. Most enzymes work best at around 30° – 40°C.

$$sugar \xrightarrow{\text{yeast}} alcohol + carbon\ dioxide$$

Carbon dioxide gives the beer its frothy head. In bread the bubbles of carbon dioxide are trapped in the dough. They make the dough rise.

Brewers and bakers add sugar or starch to feed the yeast.

Alcohol makes you drunk if you drink too much. In bread the cooking drives off the alcohol.

1 What are enzymes?
2 What substances are produced when yeast acts on sugar?
3 Cooks leave bread dough to rise in a warm place before cooking it. Why?
4 How does the carbon dioxide made when enzymes act on starch or sugar improve the bread or beer?

| yeast | catalyst | enzyme | alcohol | carbon dioxide |

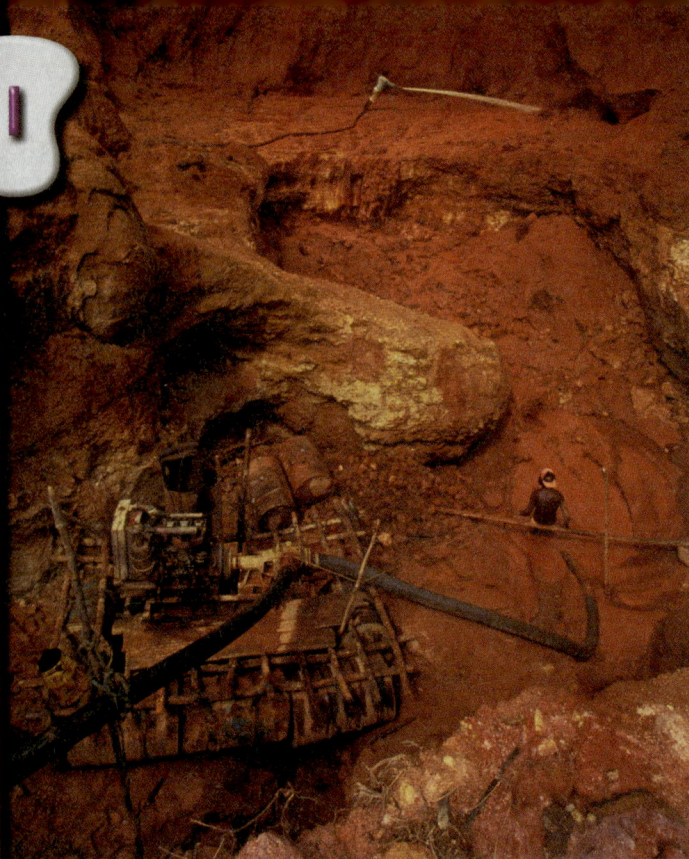

11.1 Going for gold!

This man is looking for gold. Gold is a very heavy metal. You can find lumps of it in rocks in some parts of the world. But how can you get the gold out?

One way to **extract** the gold is to grind the rocks and gold into a powder. The powder doesn't need to be very fine – something like sand will do. Now wash water through the mixture. The lighter rock particles are carried away, but the heavy gold dust settles at the bottom.

Mixtures may contain substances that are useful. To get the useful substances out, the mixture has to be separated into its different **components**. The method we use to separate out the mixture depends on the properties of the substances in the mix.

Tea leaves settle to the bottom of the teapot. The liquid tea can then be poured off the top. This method of separating a solid from a liquid is called **decanting**.

A tea bag is made of a material that lets water through but not the tea leaves. The tea bag acts as a **filter**.

Magnets are used to pull **magnetic** metals like iron or steel from a mixture. In this way food cans can be separated out from household rubbish for recycling.

1 Write a sentence that uses the word decant.
2 Gold is much heavier than rock. Explain how this helps people to find gold in a mixture of gold and rock.
3 Draw a flow chart to show how magnets could separate steel cans from plastic bottles.
4 Suggest one other way to separate plastic bottles from food cans.

| extract | components | decant | filter | magnetic |

11.2 Faking it

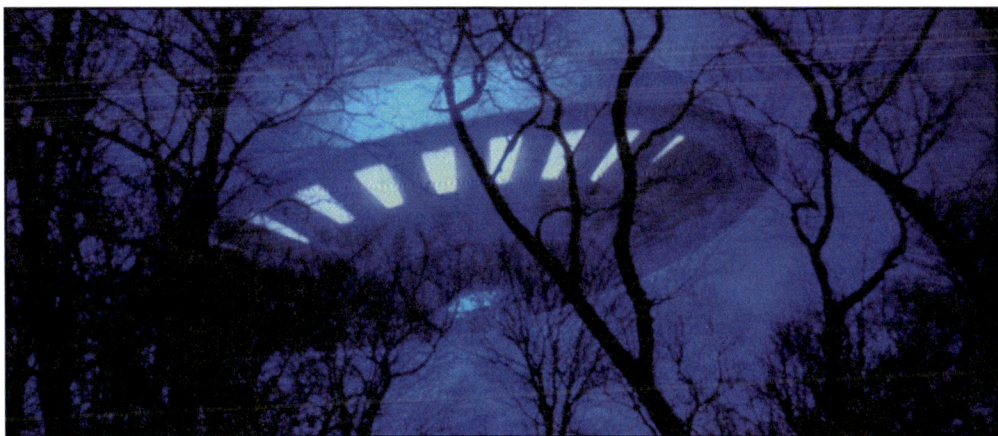

Some people claim to have found a drawing left by aliens, who visited the Earth. To find out whether or not the drawing is a fake, we can compare the ink used with Earth ink.

Most inks are mixtures of **soluble** coloured substances, which cannot be separated by filtering. **Chromatography** separates the ink mixture into the different coloured substances. The mixture should tell us where the ink came from. If the 'alien' drawing is genuine, the ink should have a different mix to Earth inks.

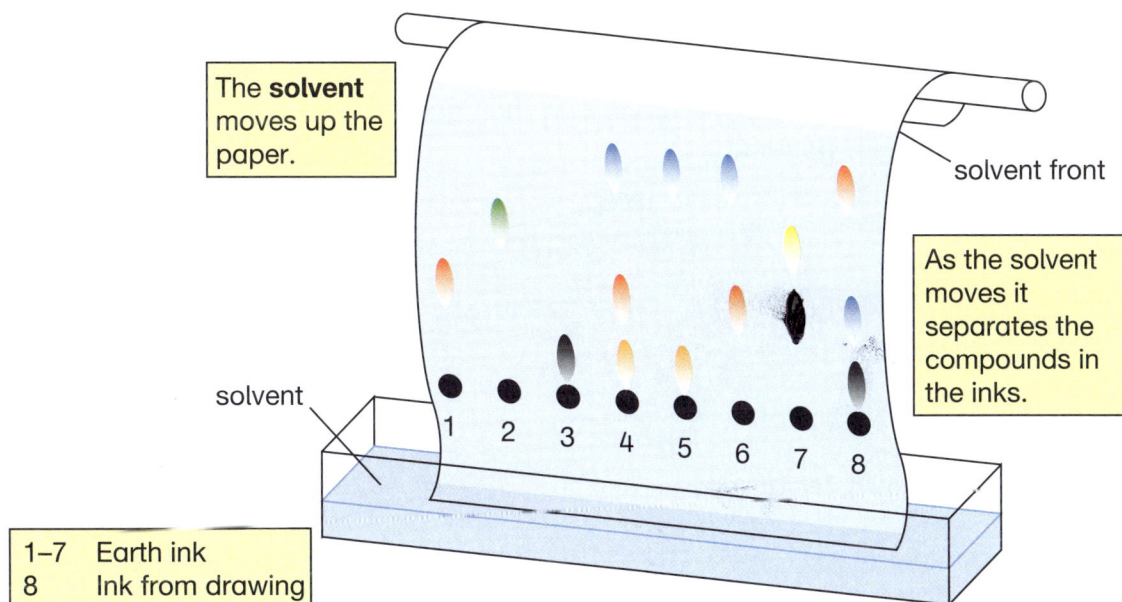

The **solvent** moves up the paper.

solvent front

As the solvent moves it separates the compounds in the inks.

solvent

1 2 3 4 5 6 7 8

1–7 Earth ink
8   Ink from drawing

1 Write a sentence that uses the word solvent.
2 Do you think the 'alien' drawing is genuine? How can you tell?
3 Name some substances that could be separated by chromatography.
4 Plan an experiment to find out if the colours of Smarties are pure substances or mixtures.

soluble	chromatography	solvent

11.3 Cleaning the blood

Blood is a very complex mixture. Doctors use a **centrifuge** to separate cells from the blood. A centrifuge spins samples of blood around very fast. The cells settle at the bottom of the tube.

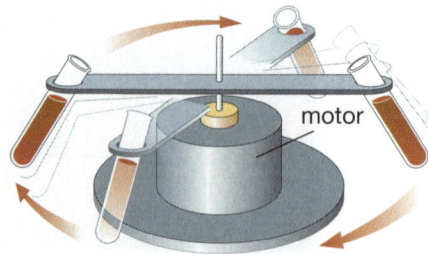

motor

The motor turns the rotary arm very fast.

Before spinning

blood cells and plasma

After spinning

clear pale yellow liquid above cells in each tube

Kidney machines use a technique called **dialysis** to wash dissolved waste from the blood. The blood is pumped along tubes made of a special material. The waste passes through the material but the rest of the blood cannot. Special dialysis solution passing the other way carries away the waste. The blood can then go back into the patient.

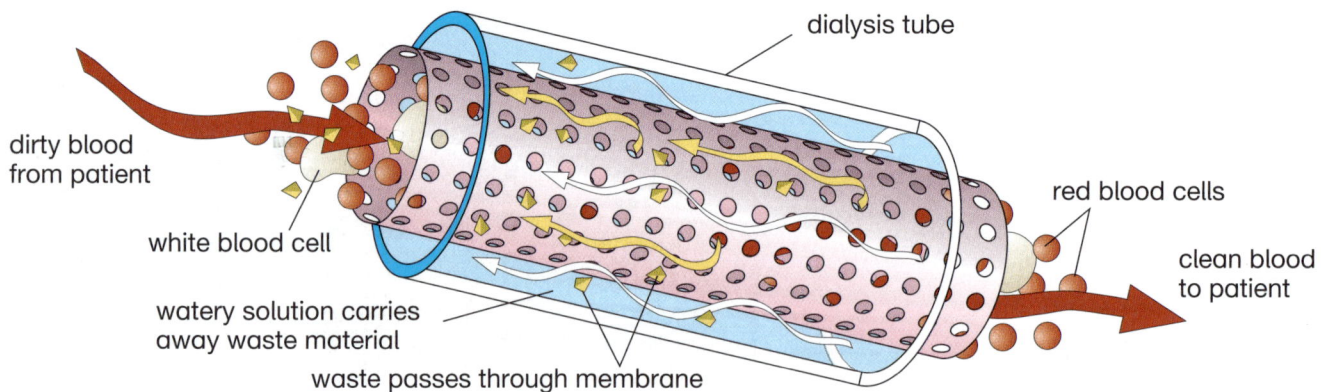

dialysis tube

dirty blood from patient

white blood cell

watery solution carries away waste material

waste passes through membrane

red blood cells

clean blood to patient

1 What do hospitals use centrifuges for?
2 Which machine in a hospital uses dialysis?
3 What does this machine do?
4 Design a leaflet to explain to patients how the separation techniques used in hospitals work. Include the separation of blood products and dialysis.

centrifuge   dialysis

11.4 Oil and whisky

Some liquids mix so well that they look like a single substance. But even these mixtures can be separated. **Distillation** is a way to separate liquids with different **boiling points**. Whisky makers and oil companies use this technique.

Whisky makers distil a mixture to produce one liquid. This liquid is a mixture of alcohol, water and flavourings with 40% alcohol. This makes it eight times stronger than most beers!

The same method is used to get drinkable, fresh water from sea water. The sea water is heated to boiling point. This causes the water to **evaporate** leaving the salt behind. The water vapour is then cooled and **condenses** to form a liquid.

Oil companies use a similar technique for **crude oil**. However, the oil companies collect more than one type of liquid from the crude oil. These different liquids are called **fractions**, which is why this type of distillation is called **fractional distillation**.

Whisky still

Whisky vapours cool in the tube and collect in the barrel.

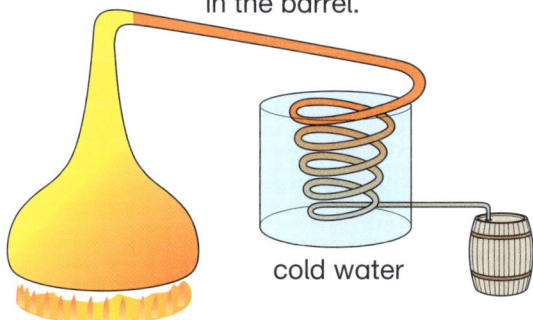

cold water

The mixture is heated to boil off the whisky.

Fractionating tower

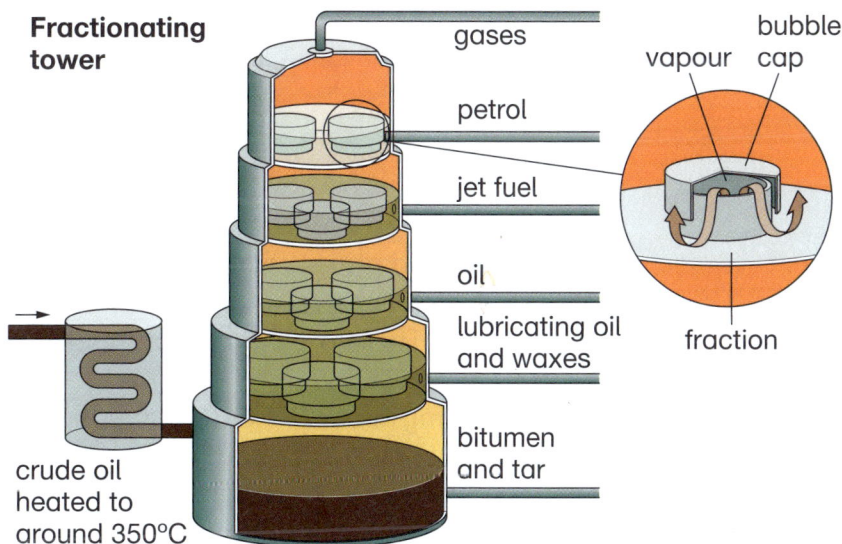

gases

petrol

jet fuel

oil

lubricating oil and waxes

bitumen and tar

crude oil heated to around 350°C

vapour

bubble cap

fraction

1 Write a sentence containing the word distillation.
2 Name two liquids that can be separated by fractional distillation.
3 What difference between two liquids does fractional distillation depend on to separate the liquids?
4 How can alcohol be separated from the water in wine? Explain why the alcohol condenses first during distillation.

distillation	**boiling point**	**evaporate**	**condense**
crude oil	**fraction**	**fractional distillation**	

12.1 Is it all rubbish?

Every one of us produces roughly half a tonne of rubbish each year. Some of this really is rubbish, but most can still be useful! It can be collected and **recycled** to make new products.

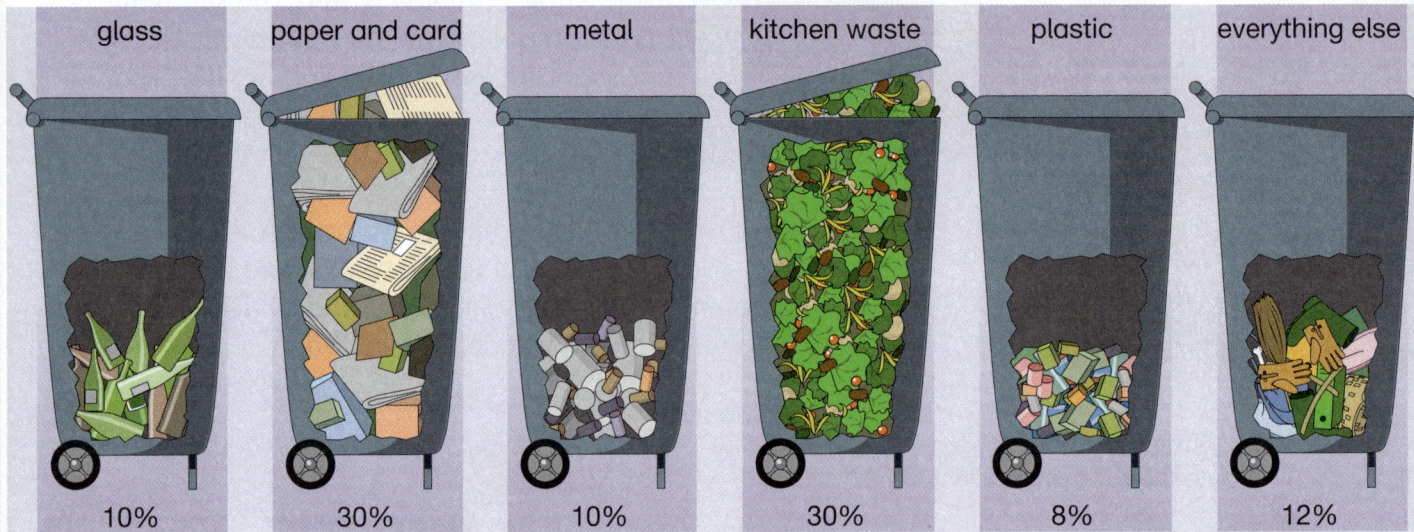

Our school's rubbish

glass	paper and card	metal	kitchen waste	plastic	everything else
10%	30%	10%	30%	8%	12%

The big problem with rubbish is that it is such a mixture of things. All the different types of rubbish need to be treated differently. Old food, kitchen waste and paper will **rot** easily. They are broken down by bacteria which feed on them. These are called **biodegradable**. Plastics, glass and metal will not rot. These are called **non-biodegradable**.

Recycling rubbish means using it to make something useful. This new product could look very different from the original rubbish. Waste paper can be recycled to make new paper or furniture, or it can be made into bricks which will burn. Some types of plastic can be recycled as fleece jackets and tops.

1 Write a sentence containing the word biodegradable.
2 Sort the rubbish in the diagram into things which are biodegradable and those which are not.
3 Draw a diagram to show the amounts of different materials in your rubbish bin at home.
4 What does recycling mean?

recycle   rot   biodegradable   non-biodegradable

12.2 What a gas!

A lot of the rubbish we make ends up in a hole in the ground. These holes are often old quarries, which are filled up and then covered with soil. They are called **landfill sites**. Who knows, you may be sitting on a landfill site right now!

Landfill sites may sound like a good idea. The rubbish is covered up and out of the way. However, we are running out of holes in the ground to fill. Another problem is that the biodegradable rubbish rots. This produces **methane gas**. The methane rises through the soil and can collect in buildings above ground. A spark produced by something as simple as switching on a light can make the methane and air mixture explode.

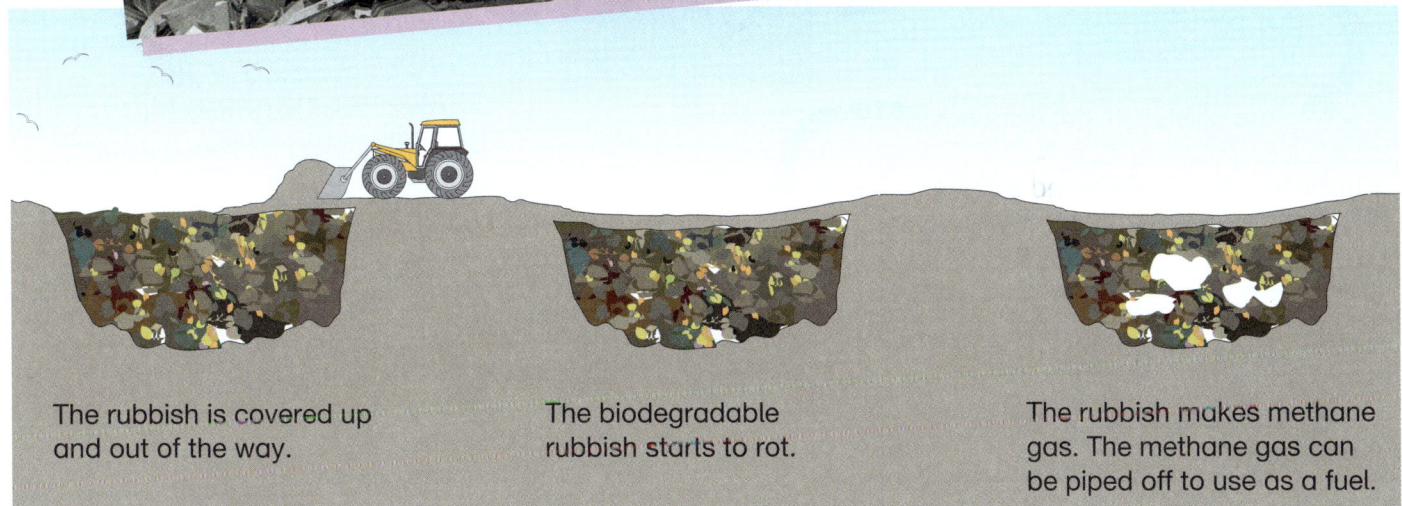

The rubbish is covered up and out of the way.

The biodegradable rubbish starts to rot.

The rubbish makes methane gas. The methane gas can be piped off to use as a fuel.

1 Which gas is produced in landfill sites?
2 What must be mixed with this gas before an explosion can take place?
3 What sort of rubbish gives off methane?
4 What sort of rubbish is safe to bury in landfill sites?
5 Methane gas has no smell. Why does this make it extra dangerous?

landfill site   methane gas

12.3 Wasting energy

We will never run out of rubbish. In fact, each year we are producing more. Rubbish could be a **renewable fuel**. Two bins of rubbish contain the same energy as one bag of coal. Burying rubbish is such a waste of energy.

Byker Reclamation Plant in Newcastle-upon-Tyne makes **fuel pellets** from rubbish. It makes 8 000 tonnes of fuel pellets each year. These can be sold for burning in solid fuel stoves.

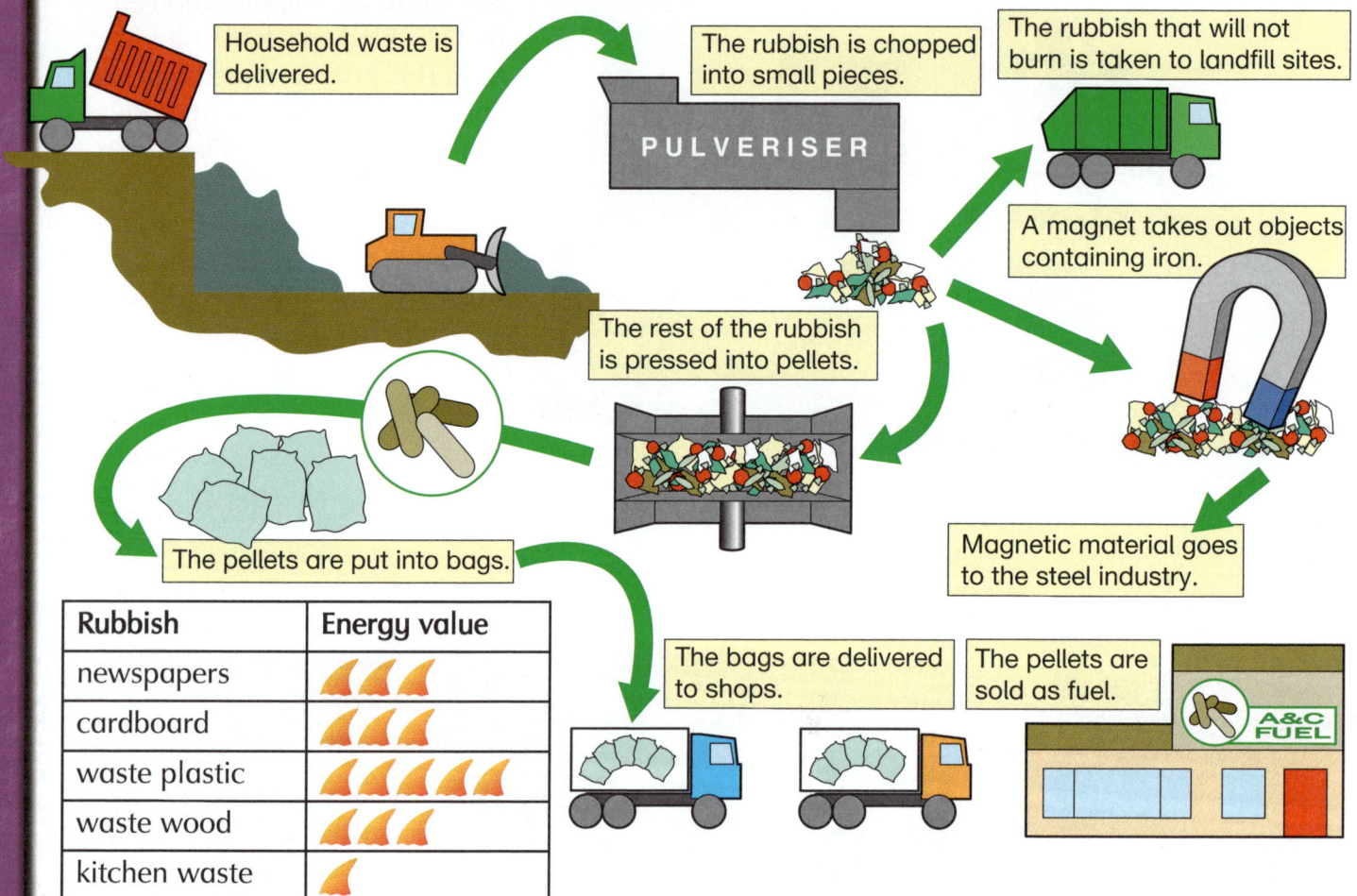

Household waste is delivered.

The rubbish is chopped into small pieces.

The rubbish that will not burn is taken to landfill sites.

PULVERISER

A magnet takes out objects containing iron.

The rest of the rubbish is pressed into pellets.

Magnetic material goes to the steel industry.

The pellets are put into bags.

The bags are delivered to shops.

The pellets are sold as fuel.

A&C FUEL

Rubbish	Energy value
newspapers	🔥🔥🔥
cardboard	🔥🔥
waste plastic	🔥🔥🔥🔥🔥
waste wood	🔥🔥
kitchen waste	🔥

1 Write a sentence using the word renewable.
2 Sort this list into things which can be used to make fuel pellets and things which cannot.
   cardboard   china   cloth   glass   metal   paper   plastic
3 Using the information in the table, draw a barchart to show the energy in different types of rubbish.

renewable   **fuel**   **fuel pellets**

12.4 Different fuels

We don't know which came first – the chicken or the egg. But we do know what comes after chickens have been around, tonnes of smelly manure! This manure makes a great fuel. It can be dried, mixed with straw and burnt. You may depend on chicken manure for your heating and cooking at home!

Chicken manure is a good example of a **renewable** fuel – it will never run out. Some fuels will run out because we are using them much faster than they are being made. These are called **non-renewable** fuels. Oil is a good example. So which is the best fuel to use?

There is plenty of **coal** in the ground and it gives out lots of heat when it burns.

We ought to look at other ways to heat our homes. What about wind, water or solar power? At least they won't run out.

Natural **gas** burns well and is clean.

Oil is a good fuel – but we ought to be careful how much we use. It will not last forever.

Rubbish pellets solve the problem of landfill sites by giving us something useful. But when they burn they still give out **ash** and **smoke.** This is an important type of **pollution**.

1 List three sources of energy that will never run out.
2 Make a list of the advantages of using rubbish pellets as fuel.
3 Now list some of the disadvantages of using rubbish pellets as fuel.
4 Draw a design for a stove that can use rubbish pellets as fuel. Show how it is different from a normal gas stove.

renewable	non-renewable	coal	gas	oil
ash	smoke	pollution		

13.1 Black, sticky and smelly!

It doesn't look like it's worth much. It's sticky and smelly and doesn't burn easily. It's also **toxic** which means it can kill living things. But this **crude oil** is one of the most useful chemical mixtures on the planet. But how do we get from crude oil to petrol for our cars?

Fractional distillation separates crude oil into different, more useful **fractions**. Oil refineries use a giant fractionating column to do this.

Fraction	Boiling point /°C	Uses
Petroleum gases	Less than 65	Bottled gas for camping or portable heaters
Petrol and diesel	75 – 150	Fuel for road vehicles
Kerosene	250 – 300	Fuel for jet engines
Lubricating oil and waxes	320 – 450	Lubricating oils help to protect engines. Waxes can be used for candles and waterproofing fabrics
Bitumen and tar	More than 500	Mixed with small stones to make garden paths and roads

1 Write a sentence with the word toxic in it.
2 Why is crude oil such a useful chemical mixture?
3 Which fraction has a boiling point in the range 250° – 350°C?
4 Give an example of a fraction from crude oil that does not burn easily.

toxic   crude oil   fractional distillation   fraction

13.2 The silent killer

Which of the pictures above shows a real murderer? Well, it's not Richard Hillman from Coronation Street! The fire is a real killer though. It burns gas made from crude oil. If it has plenty of air and is properly adjusted it is completely safe. It makes carbon dioxide and water vapour.

Gas + **oxygen** → carbon dioxide + water vapour

But if there is not enough air a different reaction takes place. This time small amounts of **carbon monoxide** are produced as well. Carbon monoxide is very dangerous. It **poisons** the red blood cells and stops them carrying oxygen to the cells of the body. Carbon monoxide poisoning can kill – and it does kill, every year.

Gas + less oxygen → carbon dioxide + water vapour + carbon monoxide

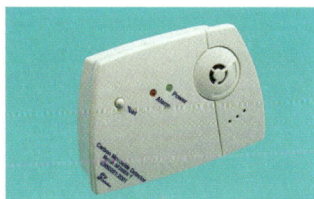

Carbon monoxide is colourless and has no smell, so you can't tell it's there. The photo shows a carbon monoxide detector. It changes colour if carbon monoxide is present, warning you to have your gas fire serviced or replaced.

1 What gas is made when fuels burn in plenty of oxygen?
2 What gas is made when fuels burn without enough oxygen?
3 What makes carbon monoxide particularly dangerous?
4 Design a poster to warn people of the dangers of carbon monoxide poisoning.

| oxygen | carbon monoxide | poisonous |

13.3 Polytastic!

True love! But does Katie know where her toy dinosaur came from? Almost certainly the **plastic** in her toy was made from crude oil in a giant **refinery** somewhere. Not quite the playful image the manufacturer was looking for!

Crude oil is the source of most plastics. Plastics are some of the most useful materials chemists have developed. Different plastics have a wide range of different **properties**. The table shows only some of the most important ones.

Properties and uses of plastics

Plastic	Important properties	Main uses
Polythene	Waterproof Does not conduct electricity Very flexible	Plastic bags and bottles
Polypropene	Waterproof Does not conduct electricity Very tough	Crates and ropes
PVC	Waterproof Does not conduct electricity Can be easily coloured	Drainpipes and electrical insulation

> Nothing is as useful as plastic. We should save all of our oil for plastic. Burning oil is a waste!

> I don't like plastic. I'd rather have toys made of wood or other natural materials. Plastics do not rot so we end up with scrap plastic everywhere.

1 What are most plastics made from?
2 Why is it useful that we can make so many different types of plastic?
3 Give one property that all plastics have.
4 Which type of plastic is used for milk crates?
5 Give one disadvantage of plastics.

plastic   refinery   properties

13.4 Big molecules from small

The beads in the Williams sisters' hair make a very simple pattern. Other people may choose to have much more colourful beads in their hair. The pattern might be planned or it may just be random. Either way, it is the collection of beads that is important not the individual beads.

Plastics are produced in a similar way. Chemists stick small molecules from crude oil, called **monomers**, together. The giant strings of small molecules are called **polymers**. 'Poly' means 'many'. That is why the word 'poly' turns up in the names of so many plastics – polystyrene, polythene, polypropylene. The reaction that joins the monomers together is called **polymerisation**.

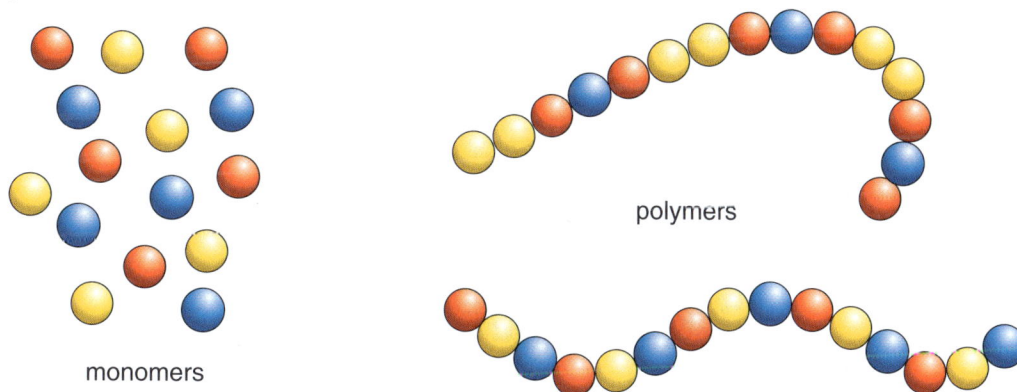

monomers

polymers

This explains why plastics have so many useful **properties**. By changing the monomers and patterns in the polymer we can change the properties of the plastic made.

1 What does the word 'poly' mean?
2 What do you think the word 'mono' means?
3 Write a sentence containing the word polymerisation.
4 Explain how we can make plastics with such a wide range of properties.

| monomer | polymer | polymerisation | properties |

Looking for patterns

14.1 Burning brightly

Chemists love to do fireworks! Very fast chemical reactions using dangerous chemicals are always fun! Many of the chemicals used in fireworks actually contain metals from a special group called **Group I**. What are these metals?

Metals in Group I are soft enough to cut with a knife and feel like modelling clay. They conduct electricity just like other metals and **react** very quickly with water – some burst into flame! When they react they give off **hydrogen** gas and leave behind an **alkaline** solution.

Chemists use the word **reactivity** to describe how quickly something reacts. Very reactive metals produce the fastest most violent reactions.

	**Potassium**: very rapid reaction, gives off hydrogen gas which bursts into flame
	**Sodium**: rapid reaction, gives off hydrogen gas which often burns
	Lithium: fizzes very strongly to give off hydrogen gas

1 List three Group I metals.
2 Which Group I metal bursts into flame?
3 Rank the Group I metals in the table into an order of reactivity. Start with the least reactive.
4 What gas does potassium give off when it reacts with water?
5 List one property that Group I metals share with all other metals.

| Group I | react | hydrogen | alkali | reactivity |
| potassium | sodium | lithium | | |

14.2 Clean round the bend!

Group I might do fireworks but **Group VII** saves lives! Group VII includes the chemicals **iodine** and **chlorine**. Both of these are used to kill **microbes** and protect us from illness.

Iodine

- Poisonous, black solid that easily forms a purple **vapour** when heated
- Does not dissolve easily in water. Dissolves in potassium iodide solution
- Very strong disinfectant, not safe to swallow even when dilute
- Cannot conduct electricity

Chlorine

- Poisonous, green gas
- Dissolves easily in water to make a **bleach** solution
- Dilute solutions of chlorine used as **disinfectants**
- Cannot conduct electricity

1 Why are chlorine and iodine useful chemicals?
2 State one thing that is true about both iodine and chlorine.
3 List two differences between iodine and chlorine.
4 What colour is chlorine gas?

| Group VII | iodine | chlorine | microbes | vapour |
| bleach | disinfectant | | | |

14.3 The boring gases

Helium, **neon** and **argon** belong to Group VIII. **Group VIII** has the most boring chemicals of all. They do nothing. Nothing at all. They are all colourless gases that do not react with anything. For this reason they are called the **inert** gases. 'Inert' means 'dead'. But just because they are inert doesn't mean we can't use them.

Helium is lighter than air. It is used in airships. It does not react with anything so it will not burn or explode. This makes it very safe.

Neon is the gas used to make neon signs. It glows with a range of colours when you pass electricity through it.

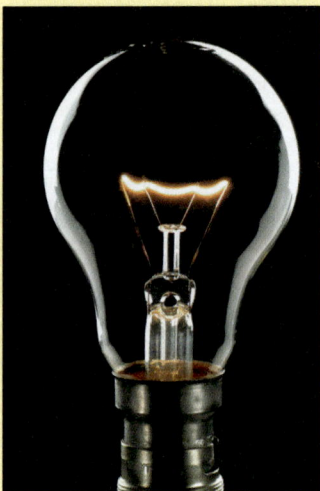

Argon is used to fill light bulbs. Argon does not react with anything so the filament in the middle of the lamp does not burn away quickly. Argon is also used to make coloured light in the same way as neon.

1 List three members of Group VIII.
2 Give two things that are true about all the members of Group VIII.
3 Why is helium better than hydrogen for filling airships?
4 Why is Group VIII sometimes called the inert gases?

helium	neon	argon	Group VIII	inert

14.4 Nice and tidy

Jenny has the messiest room ever. She claims that she can find anything that's in her room very quickly and if someone was to tidy up she'd lose things!

Scientists prefer things to be organized. There are roughly one hundred **elements** in the world. Chemists sort these elements into **groups** numbered from one to eight. Usually the group numbers are written as Roman numbers. The groups often have other names as well to tell you about the elements in them. We have looked at three of the groups:

Group number	Roman number	Name	Key facts
1	I	The alkali metals	Soft metals that react with water to give off hydrogen
7	VII	The **halogens**	Act as bleaches and disinfectants
8	VIII	The **inert** gases	Gases that don't react with anything

But why bother to organize elements into groups? Well, if you have a mystery element from Group VIII you already know that:

- it will be a gas,
- it will not react with anything, and
- it may be useful to make coloured lights.

This means that you don't have to remember everything about every element. You just need to remember which group it's in!

1 What is the Roman numeral for 7?
2 Which group contains neon?
3 Rubidium is a soft whitish metal that reacts very quickly with water. Which group does it belong to?
4 Bromine is used as a disinfectant in Jacuzzis. Which group do you think it's from?

element	group	halogens	inert

15.1 Sources and uses

This telephone box in Australia is situated in one of the sunniest places in the world. It is so remote that it uses **solar panels** to make it work. Do you think we could use solar panels in this country to power our telephone boxes?

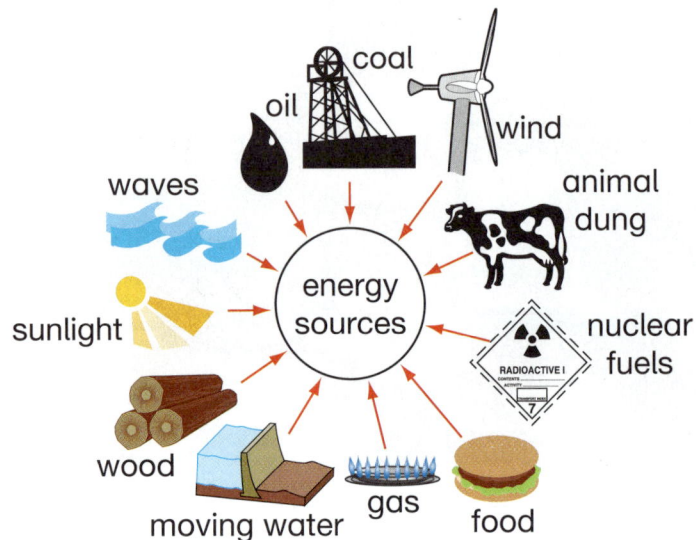

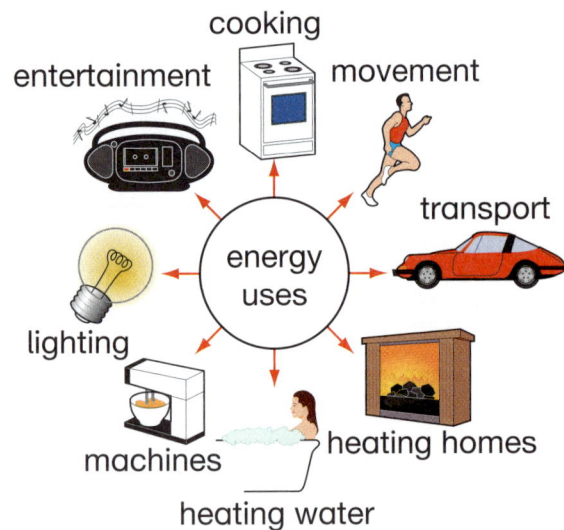

energy sources — coal, oil, wind, waves, animal dung, sunlight, nuclear fuels, wood, moving water, gas, food

energy uses — cooking, entertainment, movement, transport, lighting, machines, heating water, heating homes

Energy is needed to get things done. Energy makes people and machines work. Different things get their energy from different **energy sources**. People get their energy from the food they eat. Machines get energy from fuel or electricity. Some farms in Australia have their own electricity **generators**, which run on oil or wind power. In North Africa they use wood and animal dung for fuel.

1 List all of the energy sources mentioned on this page.
2 Sort the list into those you use and those you do not use on a daily basis.
3 Why is bottled gas useful when you go camping?
4 Why do you think that there are no gas or electricity supplies to remote areas?

| solar panel | energy | energy source | generator |

15.2 Non-renewable energy sources

Coal miners have been working in mines like this for hundreds of years to collect coal for us to use at home and at work.

Coal, oil and gas are called **fossil fuels**. They were made millions of years ago and are found underground. Fossil fuels are useful because they release **energy** when they burn.

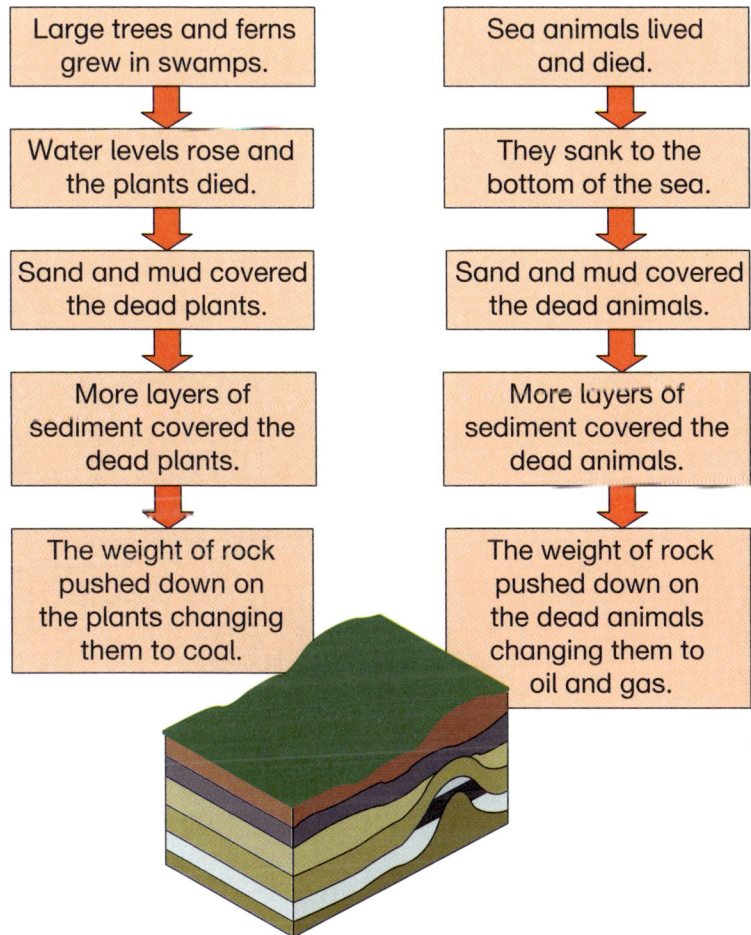

Large trees and ferns grew in swamps.	Sea animals lived and died.
⬇	⬇
Water levels rose and the plants died.	They sank to the bottom of the sea.
⬇	⬇
Sand and mud covered the dead plants.	Sand and mud covered the dead animals.
⬇	⬇
More layers of sediment covered the dead plants.	More layers of sediment covered the dead animals.
⬇	⬇
The weight of rock pushed down on the plants changing them to coal.	The weight of rock pushed down on the dead animals changing them to oil and gas.

Uranium is another fuel that is found underground. We use it in nuclear power stations to produce electricity. Fossil fuels and uranium are non-renewable. **Non-renewable** fuels are fuels which cannot be replaced. We will eventually run out of non-renewable fuels.

1 What does non-renewable mean?
2 List four non-renewable fuels.
3 Sort them into fossil fuels and nuclear fuels.
4 Which non-renewable fuels do you use at home?
5 Why can burning fuel be bad for the environment?

fossil fuels	**energy**	**uranium**	**non-renewable**

15.3 Renewable energy sources

Wind farms are becoming more and more popular as a way of creating **energy**. The 82 wind farms in the UK produce enough **electricity** to power 386 000 homes. Wind farms have to be located in remote areas because they take up a lot of space and are extremely noisy.

Energy can be created from wind, waves, tides and the Sun. None of these energy sources will run out as long as the Earth exists. These are **renewable** energy sources. The Sun can be used to heat things directly and wind can be used to turn machinery. Most renewable energy sources are used to make electricity and do not cause pollution.

1 List three renewable energy sources.
2 What do you use in school that is run on **solar power**?
3 List the advantages of renewable energy sources.
4 Give two disadvantages of wind farms.

wind farm	energy	electricity	renewable
solar power			

15.4 Waste not, want not

A great deal of heat escapes from everyone's home – heating up the cold air outside instead! This is a waste of energy and money. Energy travels from hot places to cold places. Stopping heat escaping is called **insulation**.

There are many ways houses can be insulated to ensure that as little energy as possible escapes.

Type of insulation	Where does it go?
Loft insulation made of fibre glass	Between the rafters in the loft of a building
Cavity wall insulation made of mineral wool or polystyrene beads	Pumped into the cavity between the inner and outer walls of a building
Double or triple glazing	Replaces single-glazed windows
Draught excluder made of many kinds of different materials	Under doors

1 List the things that people can do to cut down energy loss from their homes.
2 Put the list in order starting with things which save the most energy.
3 If you had to choose one method for your home which would you choose and why?

insulation   cavity wall insulation

In the balance

16.1 Chain gang

Moving boulders isn't easy! You could break them into smaller rocks and carry them, or you could use a **lever**.

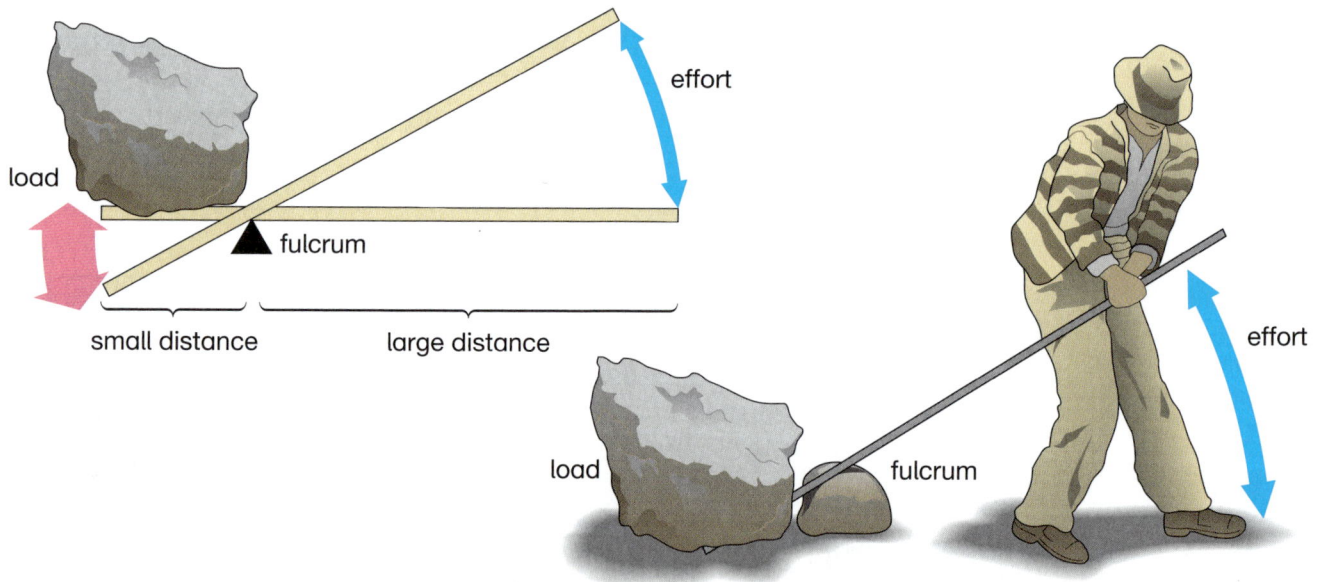

A lever is a piece of equipment that has a **pivot**, or **fulcrum**, to help move large objects more easily. When you use a lever, it turns about the fulcrum. The object you are trying to move or lift is called the **load**. The force you are using to move the object is called the **effort**.

1 What is a lever?
2 Draw a diagram of a lever to explain the terms load, effort and fulcrum.
3 Draw two levers that you would use in a garden. Label the load, effort and fulcrum in each one.

| lever | pivot | fulcrum | load | effort |

64

16.2 Super-heavyweight

The weight of a boxer is very important because it decides who the boxer is allowed to fight. A super-heavyweight would easily win against a flyweight!

One sort of weighing machine used by boxers depends on a **balance**. The boxer stands on one side of the balance and a moveable weight is on the other side. The weight can be moved closer to or further away from the **pivot**. When the beam balances, the weight on both sides is equal.

Boxer's weight	x	distance to the pivot	=	the small weight	x	distance to the pivot

Boxer's weight	x	2mm	=	1kg	x	220mm

pivot

boxer's weight

1 kg

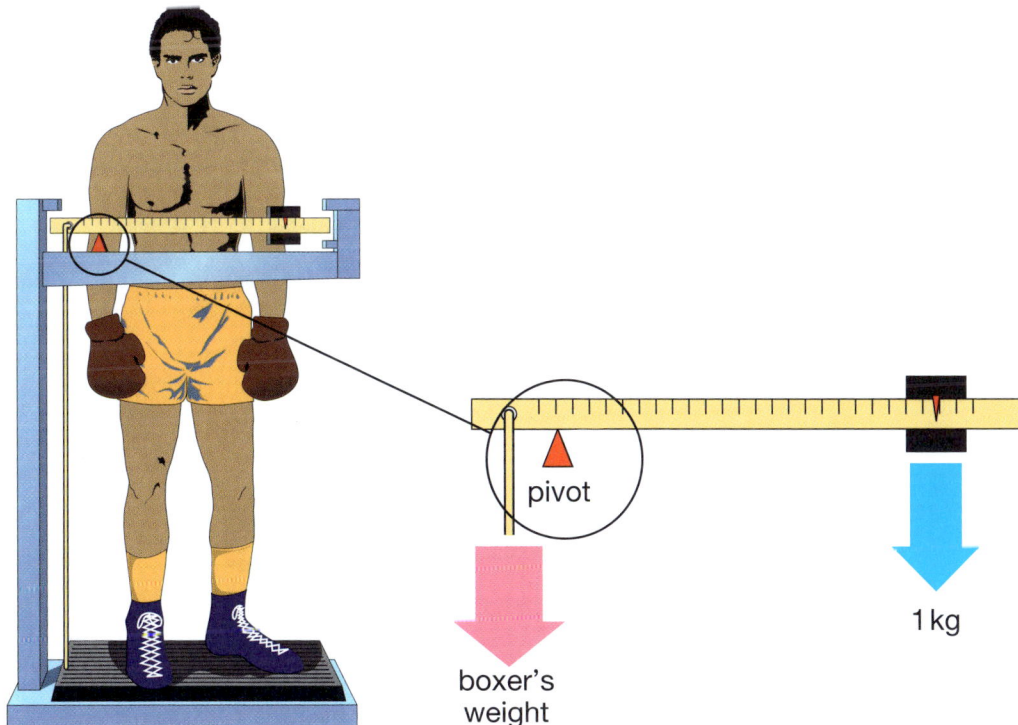

1 Work out the boxer's weight using the diagram and tables above.
2 Design a balance to weigh cake ingredients in the kitchen.
3 Design a seesaw for a park. It must be safe and allow children of different weights to play on it.

balance **pivot**

65

16.3   Down to earth

If you chose the wrong vase for a bunch of flowers, it would topple over and make a lot of mess! If something is hard to knock over, we say it is **stable**. Things that are stable usually have wide bases. They often have heavy bases too. This means that most of the **mass** of the object is low down.

What is the easiest way to carry a ladder? When the ladder is balanced it feels as if all of its mass is in one place, just above your shoulder. This point is called the **centre of mass** of the ladder. Some people use the words **centre of gravity**. This means the same as centre of mass. Anything will balance if you support it at its centre of mass.

1   Write a sentence containing the word stable.
2   Why do vases often have wide, heavy bases.
3   Why is a ladder easier to carry if you support it in the middle?
4   Design a drinking glass to be used on the fast-moving cross-Channel train, Le Shuttle.

| stable | mass | centre of mass | centre of gravity |

16.4 Bridges

These bridges are made from different materials and to different designs. However, they all do a similar job. The **pillars** of the bridges carry the **weight**. The **arches** make sure the weight is carried evenly through the pillars.

1 Draw two different designs for a road bridge.
2 Pick one of your designs and build a model of it.
3 Plan an investigation to find out the strength of your bridge. Once your teacher has checked your plan, carry it out.
4 Use the results from your investigation to improve the strength of your bridge.

pillars	weight	arches

17.1 The concert

A band will use lots of different instruments during a concert. The **sound** is very loud. You can feel the **beat** of the music in your stomach.

We make sounds in many different ways. They all depend on transferring energy. The more energy the louder the **volume**. The energy, is carried by **vibrations**. These vibrations can travel through gases, liquids and solids.

piano

double bass

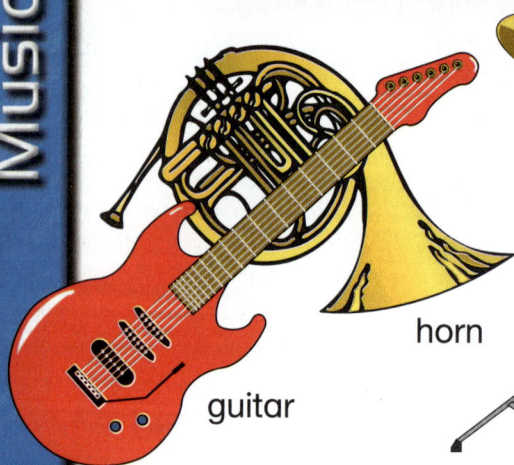

horn

guitar

cymbal

drums

saxophone

1 Make a list of musical instruments.
2 Sort your list into stringed instruments, wind instruments and drums.
3 Plan an investigation to find out how changing the length of a plucked string changes the note. If you can, carry out your investigation.

sound	beat	volume	vibration

Music machines

17.2 The recording studio

Every band wants to sign a record contract and cut a single. If they are lucky, they will go on and have a huge hit. However, most bands don't make it this far!

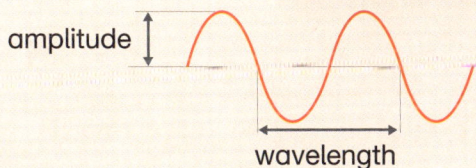

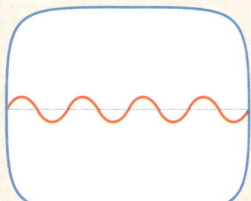
low volume

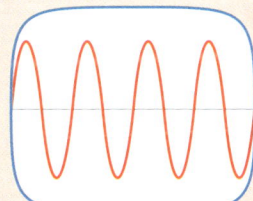
high volume

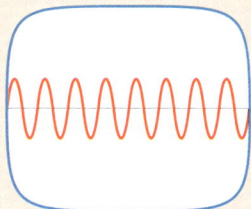
high pitch, high frequency

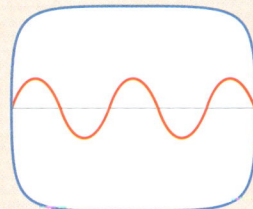
low pitch, low frequency

This machine is an **oscilloscope**. It shows sound **vibrations** as **waves**. The louder the sound, the taller the wave is. The quieter the sound, the smaller the wave is. The height of the wave is called the **amplitude**.

An oscilloscope also shows how high or low **pitched** the note is. If the note is low pitched the wave is long. If the note is high pitched the wave is short. This is called the **wavelength** of the wave. The **frequency** is the number of wavelengths that you can fit into one second. Notes with a long wavelength have a low frequency. Notes with a short wavelength have a high frequency.

1 Draw a sound wave. Label it with the words amplitude and wavelength.
2 The recording studio allows people to tour the studio from time to time. Design a brochure telling them what they might see.
3 Draw some high frequency sound waves.
4 If you were told you had a low pitched voice what would that mean?

oscilloscope	vibration	wave	amplitude	pitch
wavelength	frequency			

17.3 Whale song

You can buy recordings of dolphins and whales making noises. People claim that listening to them helps them to relax. Some parents use them to help their babies sleep.

Dolphins hear because sound travels through the water. Sound vibrations can travel through gases, liquids and solids. Space is a **vacuum**. In a vacuum there is nothing to vibrate so sound cannot travel.

Soundwaves can be reflected. We call this an **echo.** Sounds **reflect** best from hard surfaces. Bats use echoes to judge distances. Ships use **echo sounding** to find the depth of the sea.

Depth of sea = 1/2 time × speed of sound in water

sound sent out by ship

sound reflected back from sea bed

sea bed

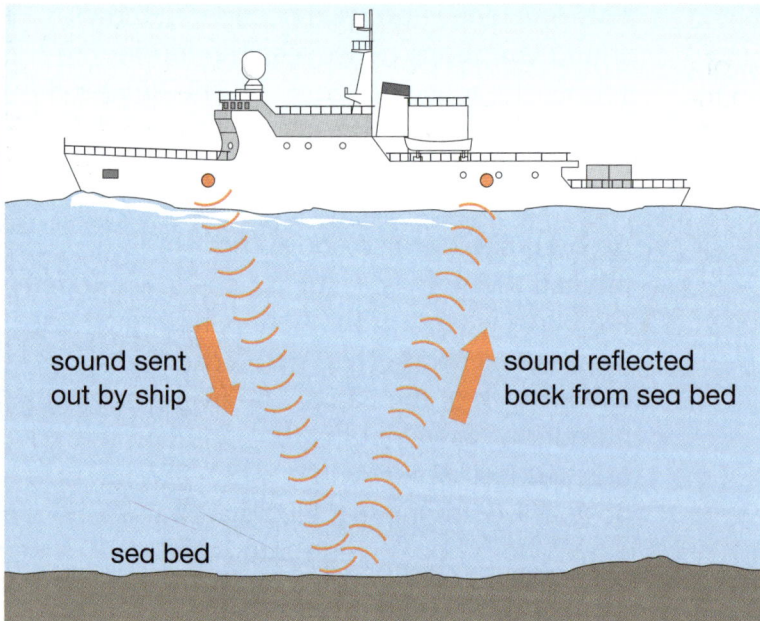

Substance	Speed of sound /m per sec
Air	330
Water	1500
Steel	5170

1 What is an echo?
2 A ship is using echo sounding to find the depth of the sea. The ship sends out a sound and receives the echo after two seconds. Using the formula above, calculate the depth of the sea.
3 Plan an experiment to measure the speed of sound in air.
4 Why does sound seem louder in the bathroom than in the living room?

vacuum   echo   reflect   echo sounding

17.4 Ears

Many people listen to music that is too loud. They stand too close to the sound system at rock concerts and listen to personal stereos at full volume. Some of them will suffer from ringing in their ears and permanent ear damage.

Very loud sounds can be harmful. After listening to loud music it takes time for your ears to recover. If the sounds are too loud for too long, the damage can be permanent. **Noise pollution** is monitored by environmental officers who work for the local council. They can confiscate the source of noise pollution.

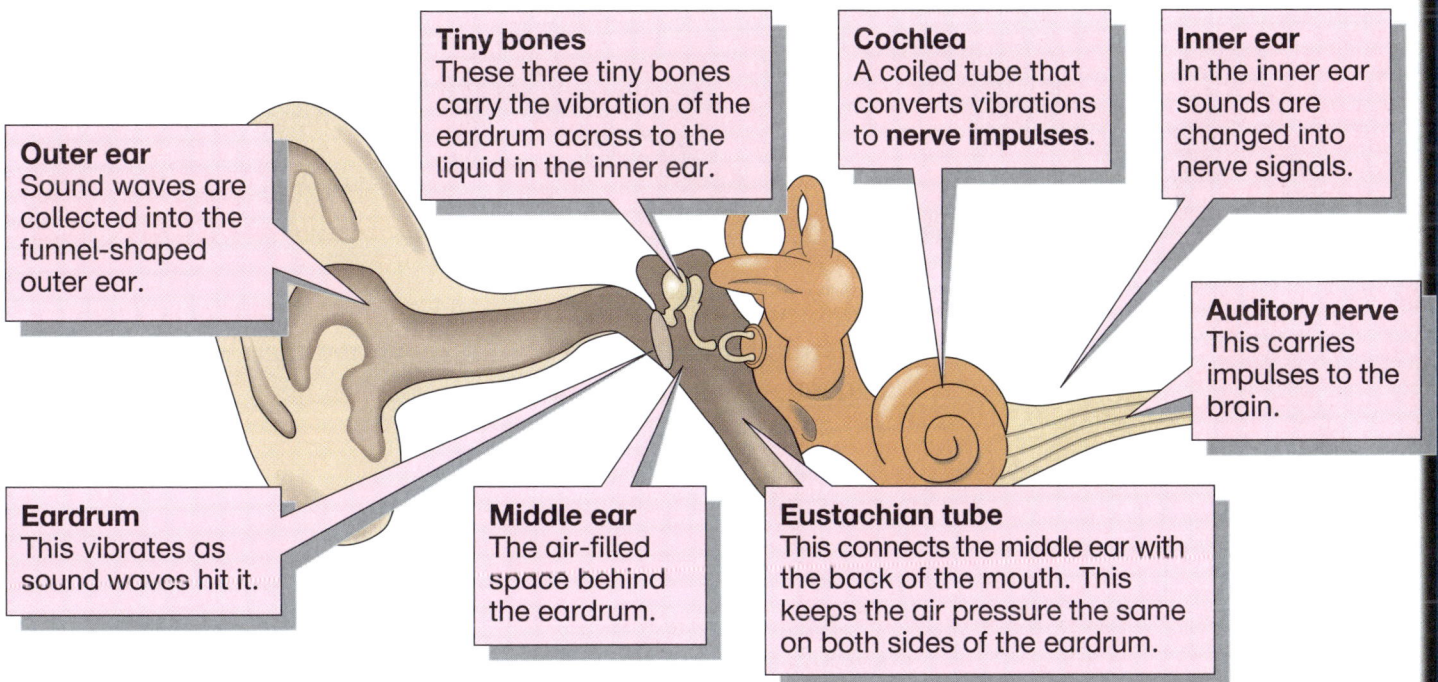

Tiny bones
These three tiny bones carry the vibration of the eardrum across to the liquid in the inner ear.

Cochlea
A coiled tube that converts vibrations to **nerve impulses**.

Inner ear
In the inner ear sounds are changed into nerve signals.

Outer ear
Sound waves are collected into the funnel-shaped outer ear.

Auditory nerve
This carries impulses to the brain.

Eardrum
This vibrates as sound waves hit it.

Middle ear
The air-filled space behind the eardrum.

Eustachian tube
This connects the middle ear with the back of the mouth. This keeps the air pressure the same on both sides of the eardrum.

1 Design a leaflet to warn people of the dangers of listening to personal stereos at full volume.
2 Why should people who work with noisy machines wear ear protectors?
3 Design a poster to show the causes and problems of noise pollution.

| noise pollution | eardrum | cochlea | nerve impulse |
| auditory nerve | | | |

18.1 Special effects

Every year hundreds of actors and stunt people are set alight by film directors! They look like they are being burnt to death, but special safety precautions make sure they are safe.

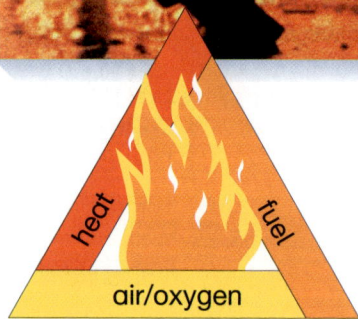

Things which burn and give out heat are called fuels. **Fuels** can only burn if they get hot enough and there is enough **oxygen**. You can put out a fire if you:
- take away the fuel,
- cut off the supply of oxygen, or
- cool the burning material down.

The different methods of putting out fires have advantages and disadvantages. Water should not be used on a fire of burning fat, such as a fire in a chip pan, because the burning fat will just float on top of the water. Water should not be used to put out electrical fires either. Many **fire-extinguishers** have foam inside them. Carbon dioxide is also used.

1 List the things a fire needs to start.
2 Why shouldn't you use water to put out a chip pan fire?
3 Make a table that shows the advantages and disadvantages of the different ways to put out a fire.

| fuel | oxygen | fire-extinguisher |

18.2 Cooking

There are many different ways of cooking a meal. At home we use cookers and **microwaves**. When you go camping, you use a portable stove or make a fire. In Africa, many people still use a fire, like the one in the photograph, to cook their meals every day.

Some heat from the fire warms the air.

Some heat from the fire goes to the aluminium foil and some goes into the potato.

Some heat goes into the tongs.

Some heat from the fire is transferred to the ground.

Some heat reaches the person.

All cookers transfer heat to food when they cook it. Gas cookers transfer **energy** from the gas as heat energy. Electrical cookers transfer electricity as heat. Microwaves use energy in waves to heat food.

Not all of the heat produced by the cooker gets to the food. Some heat warms up the cooker and some escapes into the air. Cookers which transfer most of the energy to the food are **efficient**.

1 How is heat wasted in a gas cooker?
2 List all of the ways you can cook a jacket potato.
3 Looking at your list, sort the ways to cook a jacket potato into those which waste a lot of energy and those which do not.
4 Which way of cooking a jacket potato is most efficient?

| microwave | energy | efficient |

18.3 Keeping food warm

Fast food is now more popular than ever. You can buy burgers, pizzas, kebabs and chips nearly everywhere you go.

Most take-away food is hot, so you need to keep it warm until you are ready to eat it. You have to stop heat passing out through the packaging of the food. Materials which slow down the movement of heat are called **insulators**. Plastic is a good insulator. Many insulators, such as **polystyrene** and cardboard, have small spaces within them which trap hot air. Other insulators, like aluminium foil, are shiny and reflect heat back.

Some materials allow heat to pass through them easily. These materials are called **conductors**. Metals are good conductors of heat.

1 List some materials used to package take-away food.
2 Which of these materials are insulators?
3 How do pizza delivery firms keep their pizza warm for customers?
4 Design a range of containers for baked potatoes, fish and chips and burgers.
5 Sort the materials in your list from Question 1 into a table with these headings: 'Can rot away', 'Cannot rot away', 'Recyclable' and 'Non-recyclable'. Remember that the same packaging may be written under different headings.

insulator   polystyrene   conductor

18.4 Using energy

This looks tough! The athlete is using lots of energy to move the plane. We use energy to complete everyday tasks such as getting to and from school and playing sport.

Energy exists in different forms. The main types of energy are **movement energy** and **stored energy**. Food has stored energy. Our bodies can **transfer** the energy from food and use it to move around and grow and repair our bodies. Any energy that isn't needed straightaway is stored as **fat** around our body.

Heat is often given out when energy is transferred. This is why we get hot when we exercise.

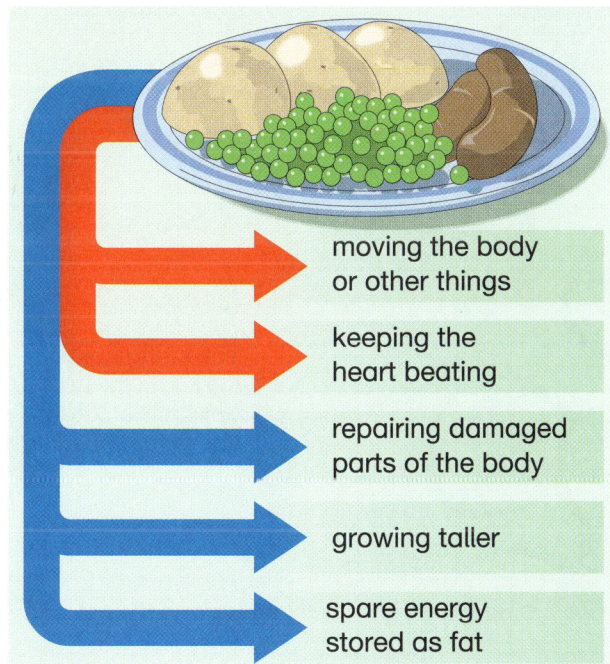

moving the body or other things

keeping the heart beating

repairing damaged parts of the body

growing taller

spare energy stored as fat

1 List all of the energy transfers your body has made today.
2 Why do you think you get hungry after a PE lesson?
3 Look at the photograph. Do you think that the athlete needs to eat more or less food than you? Why?

| movement energy | stored energy | transfer | fat |

Movement

19.1 Pushes and pulls

When the England rugby team won the Rugby World Cup in 2003, they used lots of pushes and pulls to make sure they beat the Australians in the final. These pushes and pulls are called **forces**.

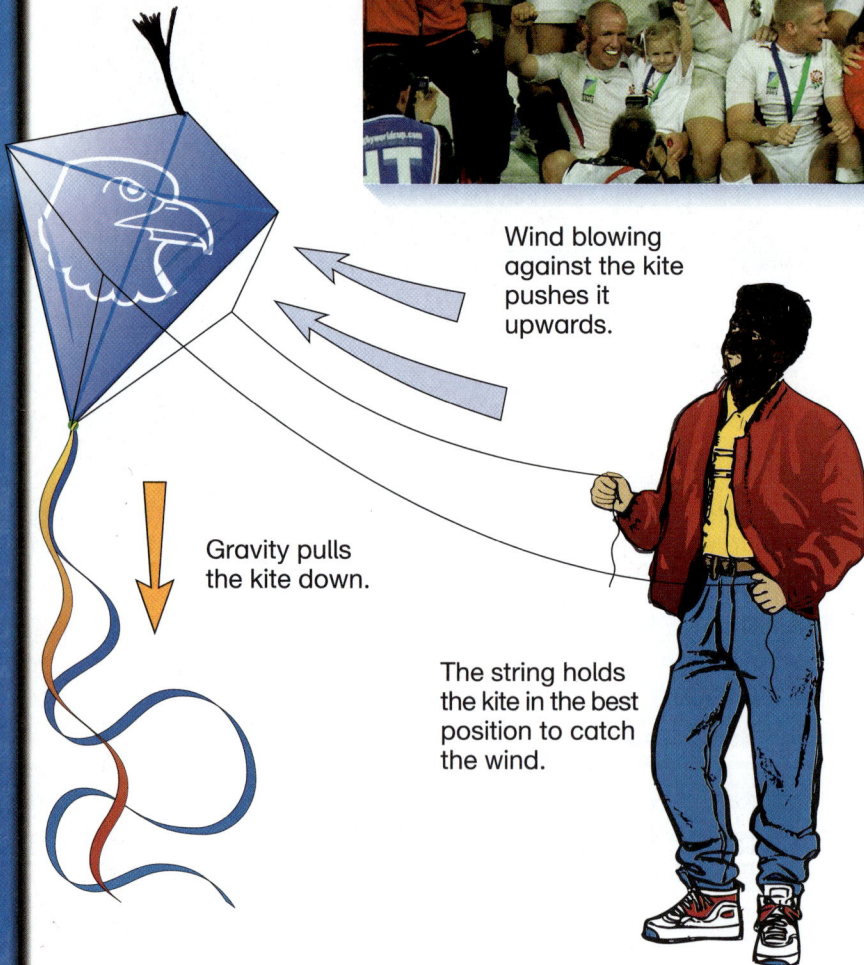

Wind blowing against the kite pushes it upwards.

Gravity pulls the kite down.

The string holds the kite in the best position to catch the wind.

Kites have a large surface area for the wind to **push** against. The person flying the kite **balances** the push of the wind by **pulling** on the kite strings. Kites need to be light so it is harder for **gravity** to pull them down. The kite stays in the same place if all of these forces are balanced.

1 Which two forces does a rugby player use most during a match?
2 What happens when two equal forces pull against each other?
3 What would happen to a kite if a person let go of the string? Why?
4 What would happen to a kite if the wind suddenly dropped? Why?
5 What would happen if you pulled too hard on the kite strings?

forces   push   balance   pull   gravity

19.2 Up, up and away

Hot air balloons are becoming more and more popular. Many people are given a balloon ride as a birthday or Christmas present. The balloons come in all shapes and sizes but they are all filled with the same thing – hot air.

A hot air balloon flys because hot air rises. A balloon pilot makes the balloon go up by increasing the temperature of the air inside the balloon. The **uplift** is bigger than **gravity**. The pilot makes the balloon go down by releasing hot air from the balloon. The uplift is now smaller than gravity. Pilots cannot steer the balloon, instead the wind **pushes** the balloon along. If there is not much wind the balloon stays still – the forces are **balanced**.

1 Which force pulls the balloon towards the ground?
2 Name the force that makes the balloon rise.
3 What must a pilot do to make the hot air balloon go higher?
4 What makes the balloon travel from one place to another?
5 What would happen to the balloon if the uplift and gravity forces were the same?

uplift	gravity	push	balance

19.3 Stopping forces

Car manufacturers spend hundreds of hours crashing new models of cars into walls. These crash tests are used to make sure that new cars are as safe as possible.

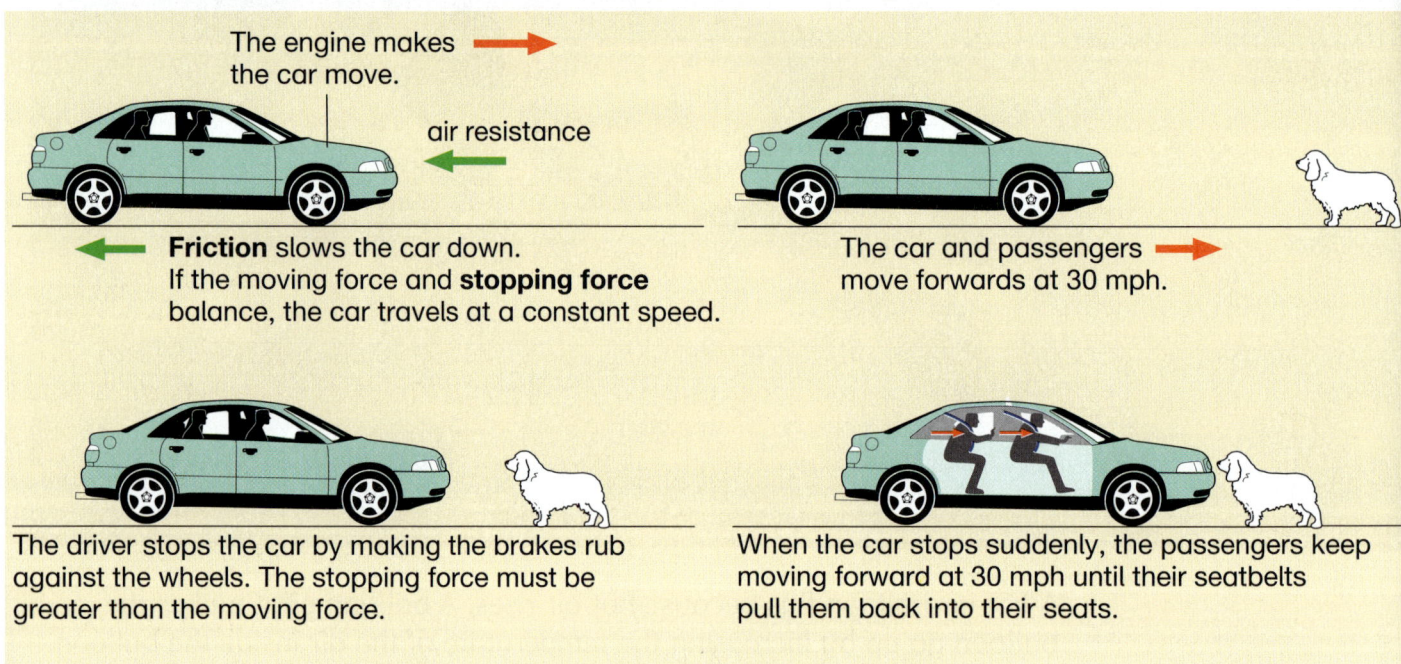

The engine makes the car move.

air resistance

Friction slows the car down. If the moving force and **stopping force** balance, the car travels at a constant speed.

The car and passengers move forwards at 30 mph.

The driver stops the car by making the brakes rub against the wheels. The stopping force must be greater than the moving force.

When the car stops suddenly, the passengers keep moving forward at 30 mph until their seatbelts pull them back into their seats.

Friction is a stopping force. **Rough** surfaces have more friction. The **brakes** of a car work using friction, they rub against the car wheels. Fast-moving objects need longer **stopping distances**.

1 What makes a car go?
2 What makes a car stop?
3 What is the name given to a stopping force?
4 What could happen if the brakes on a car become worn away?
5 Why should car and bicycle owners replace worn tyres?

friction	stopping force	rough	brakes	moving
stopping distance				

People say that there is a pot of gold at the end of every **rainbow**. Do you think this is true? Rainbows are made when light passes through tiny water droplets in the air. Every rainbow is made up of seven different colours – red, orange, yellow, green, blue, indigo and violet. You can remember the names of the colours in the rainbow by thinking of them as a **mnemonic** such as **R**ichard **O**f **Y**ork **G**ave **B**attle **I**n **V**ain.

Light is part of a group of **waves** called the **electromagnetic spectrum**. There are many different types of waves in the electromagnetic spectrum, only some of which you can see.

Other types of waves in the electromagnetic spectrum include **ultraviolet** and **infrared**. Ultraviolet means waves that are shorter than violet waves. Infrared means waves that are longer than red waves.

1 How is a rainbow made?
2 Which group of waves is light part of?
3 What does ultraviolet mean?
4 What does infrared mean?

rainbow   mnemonic   wave
electromagnetic spectrum
ultraviolet   infrared

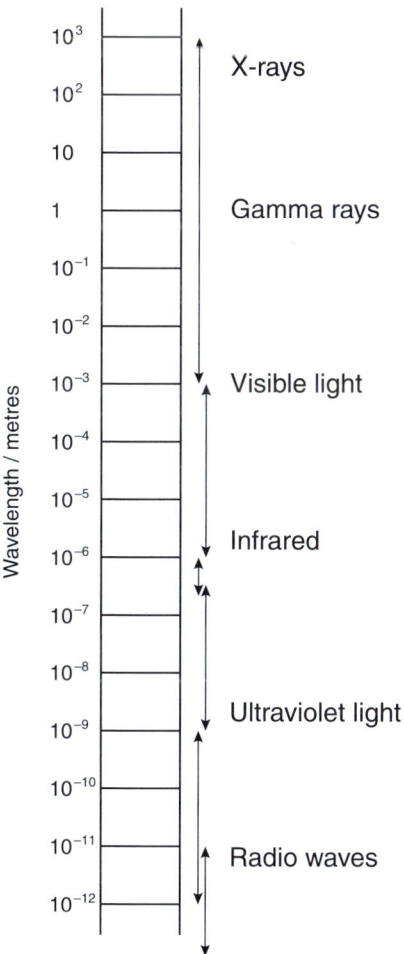

Wavelength / metres

10^3	
10^2	X-rays
10	
1	Gamma rays
10^{-1}	
10^{-2}	
10^{-3}	Visible light
10^{-4}	
10^{-5}	
10^{-6}	Infrared
10^{-7}	
10^{-8}	
10^{-9}	Ultraviolet light
10^{-10}	
10^{-11}	Radio waves
10^{-12}	

20.2 Security waves

When a burglar walks through the **infrared rays** given out by a burglar alarm, the circuit is broken and the burglar alarm goes off.

Infrared is used at home every day. TV and stereo remote controls use invisible **infrared radiation** to carry signals from the handset to the television. Electric cookers have hot-plates. They glow and give out red light. They also give out infrared rays. The infrared radiation, not the red light, heats up the food. Infrared radiation can therefore burn.

When you want to take photographs at night, you use a flash with the camera to make sure that there is enough light. Security cameras cannot use flash photography because burglars would know the cameras were there! Instead, security cameras use infrared rays to produce a good picture.

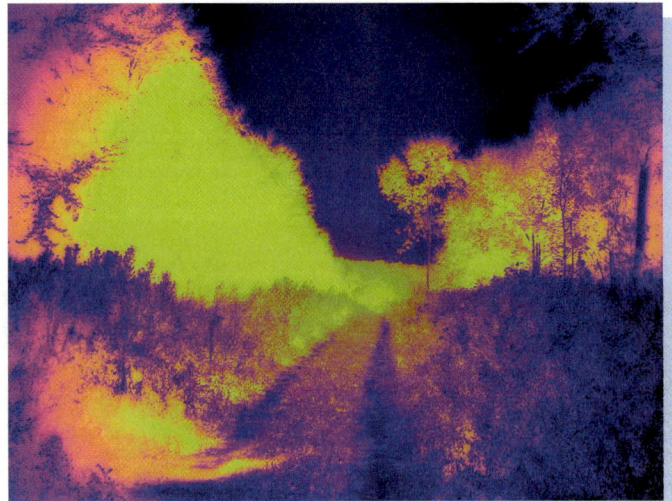

1 How does a burglar set off a burglar alarm?
2 Name three things in the home that use infrared rays.
3 Look at the two photographs. Which one was taken using an infrared camera at night?

| infrared rays | infrared radiation |

20.3 Sun and bones

Have you ever been to a disco and your shirt and teeth have glowed white? This is because an **ultraviolet light** is reflecting off your shirt and teeth!

Ultraviolet is another part of the family of waves in the electromagnetic spectrum. It has a shorter wavelength and more energy than visible light.

Ultraviolet radiation is given out by the Sun and gives us a suntan. If people spend too much time in the Sun, they can get sunburned. The skin becomes red and starts to peel. Even more exposure to ultraviolet radiation can cause skin cancer.

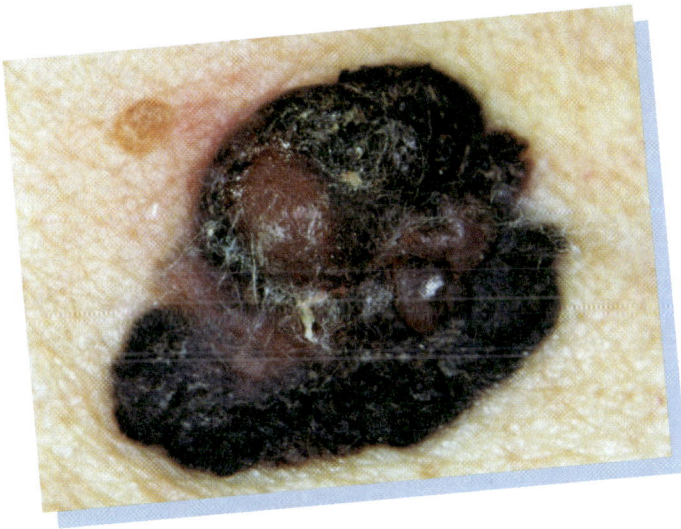

Ultraviolet light can be useful. Many people mark their videos, TVs and stereos using a special marker pen that does not show up under normal light. When ultraviolet light is shone onto their electronic equipment, the markings show up. The police can then trace the equipment if it is stolen.

X-rays have even shorter waves than ultraviolet rays. Doctors use X-rays to look at broken bones. They also use them to look at diseased lungs and objects that people have accidentally swallowed. X-rays are shone through the body onto special photographic film. The film is then developed into a black and white negative.

People who work with X-rays every day must take care to stop the harmful rays from damaging their bodies.

1   Why does your white shirt glow white in a nightclub?
2   What causes sunburn and skin cancer?
3   How can ultraviolet light help police recover stolen property?

infrared radiation   X-rays

20.4 Waves for talking, waves for cooking

When you turn on the radio, the aerial picks up waves that are sent from the **transmitter** at the radio station.

Radio waves are sent out at different frequency bands. Popular radio stations that are listened to all over the country are transmitted at **very high frequencies (VHF)**. These waves are only transmitting sound.

Television is transmitted at **ultra high frequency (UHF)**. At this frequency, sound and pictures can be transmitted.

You can use another type of radio wave to cook food, called a **microwave**. A microwave oven is lined with metal which reflects the microwaves into the food. The food absorbs energy from the microwaves and cooks.

Your mobile phone also uses microwaves to receive and send calls and text messages. Have you ever noticed your ear getting warm if you use your mobile a lot? This is because of the microwaves it is using! If you are not near a transmitter, or you are receiving interference from other transmitters, your mobile phone signal is unclear.

I   How does a radio receive sound?
2   At what frequency do televisions receive sound and pictures?
3   What type of waves do mobile phones receive?
4   How does a microwave oven cook food?

transmitter	very high frequencies (VHF)
ultra high frequency (UHF)	microwave

21.1 Radiation all around us

Background radiation is radiation that is around all the time. It comes from **radioactive** substances in some types of rock, and from outer space. Background radiation is higher in Scotland and Cornwall because of the types of rocks there.

Background radiation is even found in humans. Every day, we consume background radiation in food and water. It is also present in schools and homes. There is nowhere on Earth that you cannot find background radiation.

Some radioactive materials can be very dangerous. They can cause diseases such as cancer. Radioactive materials that are dangerous carry a warning symbol.

When radioactive materials are being moved from one place to another, great care must be taken to ensure that none of the radioactive material escapes. Special clothing also has to be worn when using radioactive materials in the laboratory or workplace.

A **Geiger counter** is used to measure levels of radiation. Every time it detects radiation entering the tube it sends an electric pulse to the counter. The number of pulses in a minute is called the count rate.

If you measured the background radiation in your classroom over a week, you would see that the count rate would be different each day. This is because radioactive substances do not give out background radiation at the same rate every day.

1 What is background radiation?
2 Where does background radiation come from?
3 Why must special clothing be worn when working with radioactive materials?
4 What do we use to measure radiation?

background radiation   **radioactive**   **Geiger counter**

Radioactivity

21.2 Three rays

Radioactive materials constantly give out radiation. All materials are made up of **atoms**. Each atom has a **nucleus** at the centre. It is the nucleus which gives out radiation. A nucleus can give out three kinds of **radioactive** ray.

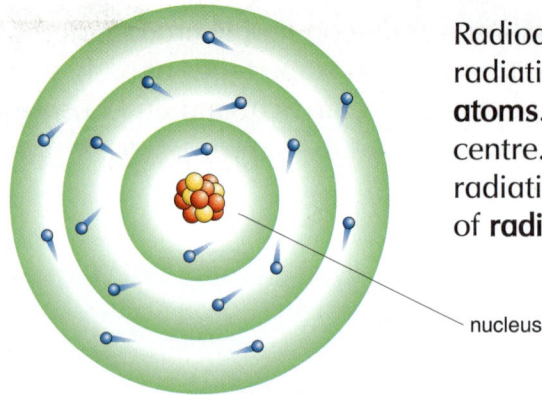

nucleus

Alpha rays

These are very fast-moving particles which can be stopped by a sheet of paper. They travel between 4 and 10 cm through the air.

Beta rays

These rays are also made up of fast-moving particles. They can be stopped by a sheet of aluminium a few centimetres thick. They travel up to 1 m through the air.

Gamma rays

This ray is an electromagnetic wave. It has the greatest penetrating power of all the waves. It can only be stopped by several metres of concrete. There is no limit on how far a gamma ray can travel.

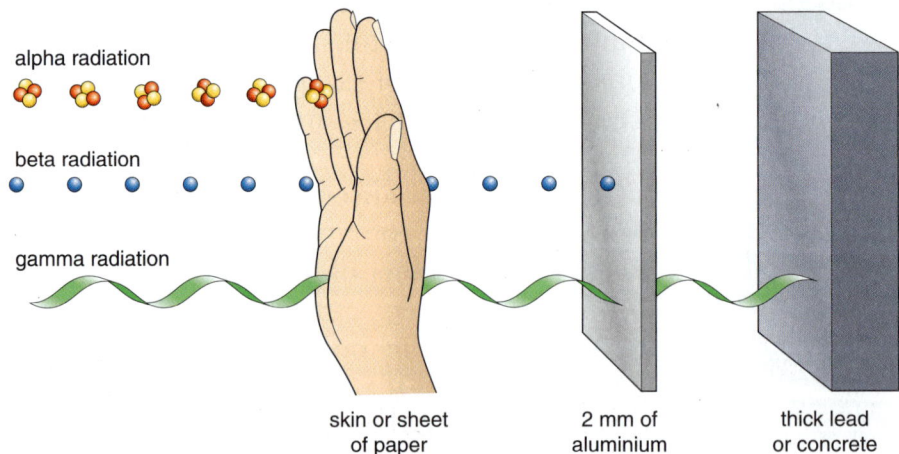

alpha radiation

beta radiation

gamma radiation

skin or sheet
of paper

2 mm of
aluminium

thick lead
or concrete

1 Which part of an atom gives out radiation?
2 What are the three radioactive rays that an atom gives out?
3 Which radioactive ray has the smallest penetrating power?
4 Which radioactive ray can travel the greatest distance?

atom   nucleus   radioactive   alpha rays
beta rays   gamma rays

21.3 Going, going, gone

Radioactive materials do not exist forever. The materials **decay** over time. Different materials take different lengths of time to decay. The time it takes for half of a radioactive material to decay is known as its **half-life.** This means that after one half-life, the radioactive material only has half of the radiation it once had.

Some radioactive materials have a short half-life. These materials are often used in hospitals to help with X-rays of the digestive system. Because these radioactive materials have a short half-life, they disappear out of the body quickly and are not harmful to the patients. Other **elements** have much longer half-lives. **Uranium** has a half-life of 4500 million years!

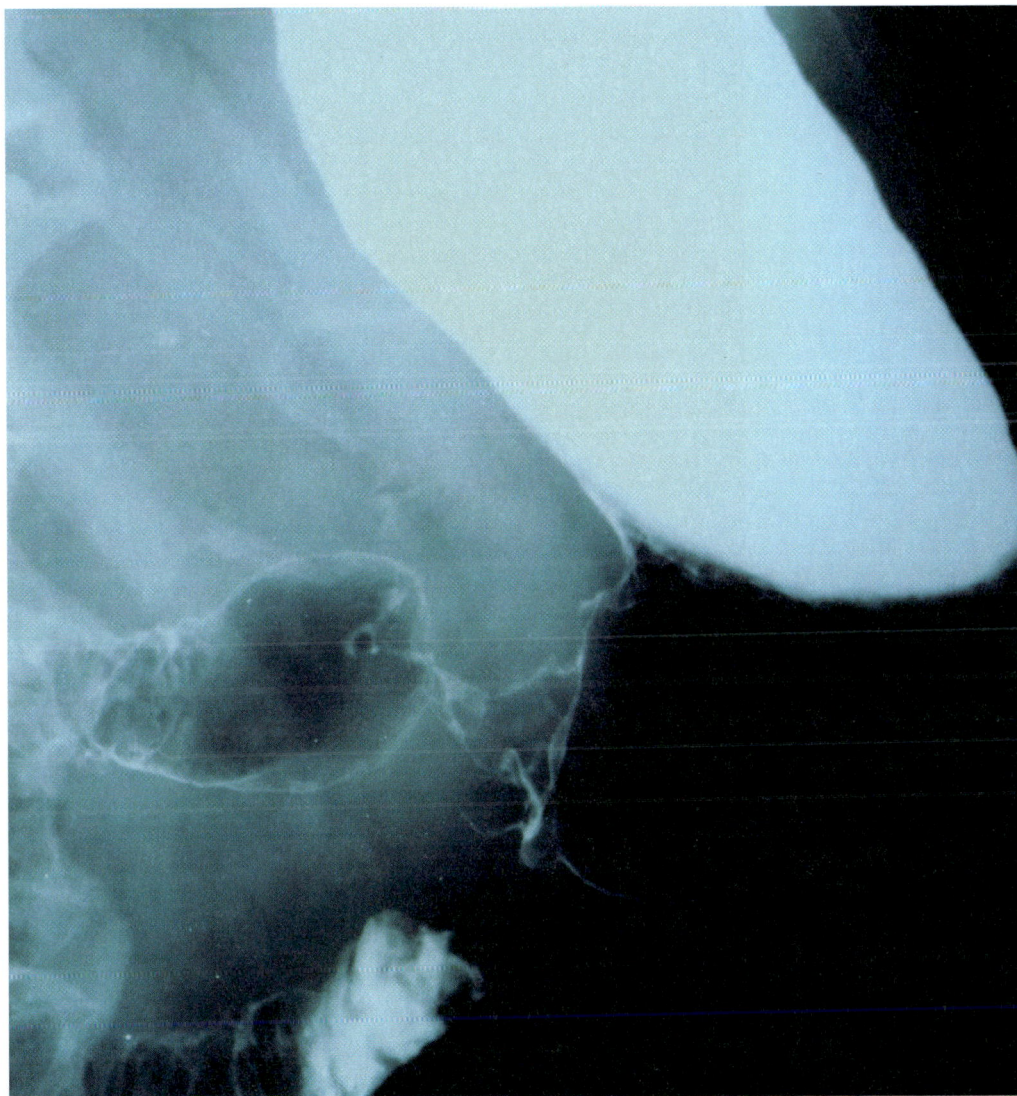

1 What does half-life mean?
2 Why would you not use Uranium to help with X-rays in a hospital?
3 Why do you think Uranium is used in nuclear power stations?

| decay | half-life | element | Uranium |

21.4 Radiation at work

The rays that are released during radioactive decay have lots of energy, which is why they can be both useful and dangerous. Although radiation can cause cancer, the energy from the rays can be used to kill unwanted cells, such as those which grow out of control to form a cancer **tumour**. Doses of gamma rays are fired at the cancerous tumour until it is destroyed.

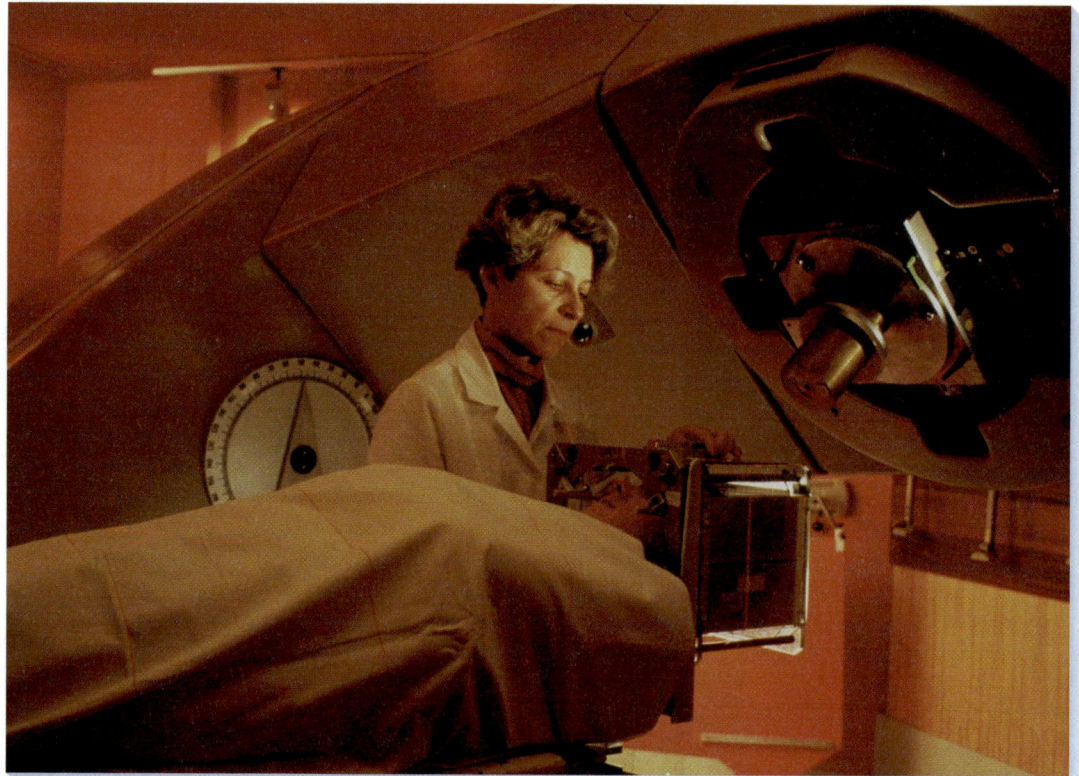

Radiation is also used to **sterilise** syringes in a hospital. When the syringes are exposed to the radiation, any bacteria on them are killed. This means that the syringes are safe to use.

Gamma rays are used on food to stop it decaying. This is called **food irradiation**. In some countries, where food transportation is slow, the food is exposed to gamma rays to kill any bacteria and so slow down decay. This does not stop the food decaying altogether. It just slows down the process.

1 How can radioactive rays help to destroy cancerous tumours?
2 Why are syringes in hospitals exposed to radiation?
3 Explain how food irradiation is helpful.

| tumour | sterilise | food irradiation |

3-D	three-dimensional
acid	a chemical that turns litmus paper red
addictive	becomes a habit
agar	a jelly made from algae that can be used for growing microbes
air sac	a very small bag found in the lungs that exchanges carbon dioxide for oxygen
alcohol	a compound found in beer, wine and spirits
algae	simple plants that live in water
alkali	a chemical that turns litmus paper blue
alloy	a mixture of two or more metals
alpha rays	a type of radiation given out by the nucleus of an atom
aluminium	a shiny, grey metal
amalgam	an alloy that contains mercury
amplitude	the height of a sound wave
amylase	an enzyme that breaks down starch
anchor	to hold in place
antibiotics	substances that fight bacteria
antibody	chemical produced by the body to attack invaders
arches	the part of the bridge between the pillars
argon	a colourless gas from Group VIII
ash	the solid left after something burns
asthma	a condition that narrows the airways
atom	the smallest part of an element
auditory nerve	carries impulses from the ear to the brain
background radiation	radiation that is around all the time
bacteria	microscopic living things
balance	1 being able to stand up without falling over, knowing which way up you are
	2 a simple weighing machine
	3 to equal out
beat	musical rhythm
beta rays	a type of radiation given out by the nucleus of an atom
biodegradable	can be broken down by bacteria
bleach	a cleaning chemical that kills germs and removes stains
boiling point	temperature at which something boils
brakes	rubber pads that grip wheels to slow or stop vehicles
brewing	the process of making beer
bronchitis	a lung infection where the bronchioles become painful
bud	the part of a plant that contains a new flower
by-product	something produced by a reaction that is not the main product
cancer	a disease where new cells form abnormally creating a tumour
carbon cycle	the movement of carbon through the food chain and to and from the atmosphere
carbon dioxide	a colourless gas that is found in very small amounts in the air; gas produced during respiration
carbon monoxide	a poisonous gas produced when natural gas burns without enough oxygen
carnivore	a meat-eating animal
casualties	people injured in an accident, war or fire
catalyst	a substance that speeds up a reaction without being used up
cavity wall insulation	a type of insulation that is used to fill the cavity in house walls
cement	a grey powder that is one of the ingredients of concrete
centre of mass and centre of gravity	the point at which the weight of an object seems to be concentrated
centrifuge	a machine that spins mixtures around very fast to separate them
chemical reaction	when two or more chemicals react together and bring about a change
chemically	using chemicals
chlorine	poisonous, green gas from Group VII
chromatography	a method of separating dissolved substances
chromosome	a long string of genes found in the nucleus of cells
clay	fine-grained mud used to make bricks and pottery

clone	an organism that is genetically identical to another organism
coal	a fuel that gives out heat when it burns
cochlea	coiled tube in the ear that converts vibrations to nerve impulses
colour deficiency	an inherited disease
combustion	burning
components	parts
composite	a material that contains two or more different substances
condense	to change from a gas or vapour to a liquid
conduct	to let electricity or heat through
conductor	a material that lets electricity or heat flow through it
crossbreeding	breeding two different species together to produce a new species
crude oil	unrefined oil
crystal	a pure piece of mineral with sharp edges and a regular shape
cutting	a small piece of a plant that can be used to produce a new, cloned plant
cystic fibrosis	an inherited disease
decant	to pour off the liquid, leaving behind the solid
decay	break down
decomposition	when something breaks down or rots
density	a measure of how heavy something is
desert	a very dry area of land
detect	notice that something is there
dialysis	a way to remove dissolved waste from the blood
diamond	a very hard mineral
disinfectant	a cleaning chemical that kills germs
dispersal	when seeds are carried away from the parent plant
dissolve	to disappear into a liquid
distillation	a way of collecting a pure liquid from a mixture
dominant	a gene that controls how you look
dormant	alive but appears to be asleep; a dormant volcano is one that has not erupted in a long time
DNA	a chemical that carries genetic information
eardrum	thin vibrating layer between the outer and middle ear
echo	when soundwaves are reflected
echo sounding	when ships send out soundwaves to measure the depth of the sea
efficient	does not waste energy
effort	the force you are using to move something
electricity	energy that flows through wires
electromagnetic spectrum	the group of electromagnetic radiations
element	substance containing only one type of atom
enamel	a very hard substance that teeth are made from
energy	the ability to do something
energy source	something that gives out energy
engulf	to swallow up
environment	the world that surrounds us
environmentally friendly	something that does not damage the environment
enzyme	a substance that changes the rate of a reaction
erupt	throw out lava, rocks and hot gas
estuary	where a river meets the sea
evaporate	change from a liquid to a gas
extract	take out of something else
fat	chemical that gives energy and warmth
fermentation	a chemical reaction that occurs when yeast feeds on sugar and changes it to alcohol
fertiliser	a chemical used to increase plant growth
fertility treatment	treatment with hormones to increase the chances of having a baby
filter	to pass a mixture of a liquid and a solid through a sieve to separate them
fire extinguisher	portable device for extinguishing fires
flowers	contain the reproductive organs of a plant
food chain	a diagram to show what different species eat
food irradiation	using radiation to kill any bacteria on food and slow down decay

food web	a complicated food chain
force	push or pull
fossil fuel	a fuel made from the remains of decayed animals and plants compressed over millions of years
fraction	liquid collected from crude oil after fractional distillation
fractional distillation	a method of separating liquids by boiling points
frequency	the number of wavelengths in one second
friction	a rubbing force which produces heat and wear and tear
fruit	the part of a plant that contains the seeds
fuel	a substance that gives out heat when it burns
fulcrum	the balance point for a lever; another word for pivot
fungi	plants that cannot make their own food
gamma rays	a type of radiation given out by the nucleus of an atom
gas	not liquid or solid, a gas spreads out to fill all of the available space
Geiger counter	an instrument used to measure levels of radiation
gene	contains the information for particular characteristics
generator	a machine that produces electricity
genetic engineering	changing the genes in a cell
germination	when a seed begins to grow
glucose	a type of sugar, used in respiration
granite	a type of igneous rock
graphite	a form of carbon
gravity	a force which pulls objects towards the Earth
grinding	crushing something into a powder
group	a column of the Periodic Table
Group I	the alkali metals
Group VII	the halogens
Group VIII	the inert gases
haemophilia	an inherited disease
half-life	the time taken for half of a radioactive material to decay
halogens	elements from Group VII
heart disease	when the heart cannot work properly
helium	a colourless gas from Group VIII
herbivore	a plant-eating animal
hormones	chemical messengers produced by glands in the body
humus	decayed remains of plants and animals found in the soil
hydrogen	a colourless gas
identical	the same as something else
igneous	a type of rock made when magma or lava cools
illusion	something that looks different from what it really is
inert	unreactive
infrared	waves that are longer than red waves, part of the electromagnetic spectrum
infrared radiation	infrared waves
infrared rays	thin lines of infrared waves
inhaler	a container of chemicals taken by asthmatics to help them breathe
inherited	passed on to you from your parents
insulation	stops heat escaping
insulator	a material that does not let electricity or heat flow through it
iodine	poisonous, black solid from Group VII
key	used by biologists to identify organisms
lactic acid bacteria	special bacteria used to produce yoghurt
landfill site	a hole in the ground where waste is dumped and then covered with soil
laom	garden soil containing a good mix of sand, clay and dead plant material
lava	hot, liquid rock flowing along the surface of the Earth
lead	a heavy, grey metal
leaves	the part of a plant that makes food
lever	a simple machine, like a see-saw, that has a fulcrum in the middle
limestone	a sedimentary rock made underwater from the remains of tiny animals or chemical deposits
lipase	an enzyme that breaks down fats

lithium	a Group I metal
load	the object you are trying to move or lift with a machine
lock and key model	a model that explains how enzymes work
lungs	organs in the chest that exchange carbon dioxide for oxygen
magma	hot, liquid rock found underground
magnetic	an object attracted to a magnet
marble	a metamorphic rock
mass	the amount of material in an object, measured in kilograms
menstrual cycle	monthly loss of blood that occurs in women after an unfertilised egg is lost from the body, commonly called a period
mercury	a liquid, silvery metal
metamorphic	a type of rock made when heat and pressure act on other rocks
methane gas	a gas made when plants and animals rot
microbe	a micro-organism
micro-organism	a tiny organism
microscopic	so small that it can only be seen with a microscope
microwave	1 an oven that cooks food very quickly with radiation waves
	2 a type of radio wave used to cook food
minerals	1 substances needed by the body in very small amounts
	2 chemicals that form part of a rock
mnemonic	something that helps you to remember, such as a verse
monomer	a small molecule that can be joined in a chain to make a polymer
mortar	a substance used to join bricks together
mould	very small fungi
movement energy	energy used to move around, grow and repair our body
mudstone	a sedimentary rock made from small grains of mud pressed together
neon	a colourless gas from Group VIII
nerve impulse	signal that passes along nerves
neutral	neither acid nor alkaline
nicotine	an addictive chemical found in tobacco
noise pollution	when a sound is offensively loud
non-biodegradable	cannot be broken down by bacteria
non-metal	a material that is not a metal
non-renewable	cannot be replaced
nucleus	1 the part of the cell that controls all of the cell's functions
	2 the centre of an atom
nutrients	important foods
oestrogen	female sex hormone
oil	a thick, greasy liquid made from plants or animals for fuel or food
organism	a living thing
oscilloscope	a machine that shows sound vibrations as waves
ovary	the female reproductive organ which produces eggs
ovulation	release of an egg from the ovary
oxygen	a colourless gas needed for respiration
packaging	materials used to contain or protect something
passive smoking	when someone does not smoke but inhales smoke from someone else's cigarette
penicillin	a drug that kills bacteria
photosynthesis	a chemical reaction in plant cells which produces energy from light and carbon dioxide
pillars	the vertical 'legs' of a bridge
pitch	how high or low a musical note is
pivot	the balance point of a lever; another word for fulcrum
plastic	an artificial material often made from oil
plates	the pieces that make up the surface of the Earth
poisonous	can make you ill or kill you
pollutants	waste materials and chemicals that pollute the environment
polluted	spoilt by waste materials
pollution	when waste materials spoil the environment
polymer	a large molecule made up of many small molecules

polymerisation	making polymers from monomers
polystyrene	a type of plastic
potassium	a Group I metal
pressure	force produced by pressing
preventer	a type of inhaler that reduces swelling in the airways
producer	an organism that can make its own food
progesterone	female sex hormone
properties	a characteristic that belongs to something
protease	an enzyme that breaks down protein
protector	a type of drug prescribed for asthmatics
protein	a chemical needed by the body for growth and repair
pull	a force that brings things together
push	a force that moves things apart
radioactive	gives out radiation
rainbow	the colours of the spectrum displayed in the sky
react	1 take part in a chemical change
	2 to respond to a stimulus
reaction	1 a chemical change
	2 a response to a stimulus
reactivity	how easily a chemical reacts
recessive	a type of gene that does not control how you look
recycle	use to make something new
refinery	a factory that makes products from crude oil
reflect	to bounce light or sound back
reinforced	made stronger
reliever	a type of inhaler that relieves the symptoms of asthma
renewable	able to be replaced
resin	a type of plastic
respiration	a chemical reaction that releases energy from food
reusable	can be used again
roots	anchor plants in the soil, take up water and minerals
rot	break down
rough	bumpy, not smooth
rust	chemical reaction between iron, water and air which leaves a reddish-brown coating
sandstone	a sedimentary rock made from grains of sand pressed together
SARs	a respiratory disease that is spread in the same way as flu
seaweed	large algae that live in the sea
sedimentary	a type of rock made from tiny grains of material pressed together
seeds	contain a new plant
selective breeding	breeding plants or animals with a particular purpose in mind
sensation	feeling
sensory nerves	nerves which carry impulses from the sense organs to the brain
smoke	fine powdered solids in the air
sodium	a Group I metal
soil	material in which plants grow
solar panel	a device that uses energy from the Sun to produce electricity
solar power	energy from the Sun
solder	an alloy of tin and lead with a low melting point
soluble	will dissolve
solution	a liquid which has a substance dissolved in it
solvent	a liquid which can dissolve a solid
sound	what you hear
stable	hard to knock over
starch	an insoluble carbohydrate
stem	supports the leaves and flowers of a plant
stereoscopic	seeing two slightly different images as one 3-D image
sterilise	remove any bacteria
stimulate	encourage something to begin
stopping distance	the distance covered by an object when it is in the process of stopping

stopping force	a force that stops an object moving
stored energy	energy that is stored as fat around our body
sugar	used during respiration to produce energy, found in many foods
swamp	a waterlogged area
symptom	a sign that something is wrong
tar	a thick, black substance found in cigarettes
taste buds	small organs on the tongue that can taste substances
temperature	a measure of how hot something is
tin	a metal with a low melting point
tobacco	a plant used to make cigarettes
toxic	poisonous
transfer	change from one thing to another
transmitter	sends out radio waves
turbidity	suspended particles of dirt in ponds and streams that reduce plant growth
tumour	a group of cells that have grown out of control
ultra high frequency	frequency at which sound and picture waves can be transmitted
ultraviolet	waves that are shorter than violet waves, part of the electromagnetic spectrum
uplift	upward force in air or water
Uranium	a non-renewable, nuclear fuel
vacuum	a volume of space where there are no particles
vapour	particles of moisture suspended in the air
very high frequencies	frequencies at which sound waves are transmitted
vibration	moving back and forth by tiny amounts very quickly
volcano	a place on the surface of the Earth where hot, melted rock comes out
volume	how loud something is
waterlogged	soil that has too much water in it
wave	something that rises and falls as it moves; the form in which sound travels
wavelength	the length of one wave
weight	how heavy something is
weld	to join two metals by melting them together where they meet
white blood cells	colourless cells in the blood that protect the body from disease
wind farm	large group of wind-driven generators
windpipe	the tube that takes air from your mouth to your lungs
X chromosome	a sex chromosome that decides if we are male or female
X-rays	part of the electromagnetic spectrum, used in hospitals to look at broken bones
yeast	tiny, single-celled fungi used in brewing and baking
yoghurt	a food made from milk
Y chromosome	a sex chromosome that decides if we are male or female